2
0
1
8

PROJECT IMPACT

REPORTS

THE
GUMPERT
FOUNDATION

Dialogues In Action
408 NW 12th Ave, Suite 506
Portland, OR 97209
503.329.4816
dialoguesinaction.com

Table of Contents

Introduction   **5**

PeopleShores   **11**

Ronald McDonald House Charities of Southern California   **37**

San Diego Children's Choir   **55**

Pro Kids | The First Tee of San Diego   **75**

Venice Family Clinic   **89**

Words Alive   **113**

Appendix   **139**

Introduction to the Project

The aim of Project Impact is to develop in nonprofits the ability to do credible self-studies of their impact.[1] As such, this is a capacity-building project. The reports in this compendium are written by the teams from nonprofits and social enterprises and represent the findings from their data collection and analysis.

The development of evaluation capacity takes time and iteration. It requires both instruction and practice – training in some of the leading techniques of research accompanied by ongoing applications and practice. This project recognizes the power of partnership, the enrichment of cross-pollination of ideas among like-minded organizations, the durable impact of a learning community, and the potential inspiration for a sector when exemplars are developed and elevated.

Project Impact takes teams of leaders from nonprofits through a process of discovery about the power of evaluation. The idea is to develop the ability to see and communicate the effects of the programs on the

---

1 This project is primarily focused on developing the ability of staff teams to implements self-studies about the effects of their programs. It is not designed to provide an experimental or quasi-experimental version of impact evaluation. Instead, it is an effort to upgrade the existing capability of each organization and give them tools to gather data on the attributed impact both qualitatively and quantitatively from the subjects they serve.

people they are designed to serve. There are three primary movements to the project: (1) Intended impact, (2) Inquiry, and (3) Implication.

Project Design

The project begins with a focus on the work of identifying and clarifying the intended impact of each of the participating programs. Once the ideas have been developed and indicators identified, the teams then design a questionnaire to collect data about quantitative measures and a qualitative interview protocol to collect qualitative data. These data are analyzed. Themes are identified and then translated into findings. From the findings, the teams develop program responses and communiques of their impact.

The fundamental elements of the Project Impact follow an arc of evaluation design:

Part 1 - Intended Impact

This project begins with the identification and clarification of what effects are intended through the work of each of the projects. Each team develops an articulation of intended impact to include the components necessary for evaluation design.

A. Main Ideas of Impact

Each team identifies and crafts ideas of impact to frame the intention of direct impact for the program. In some cases, these ideas are mapped in relation to the secondary and tertiary impacts of the program to gain clarity about the fundamental notions of desired effect as a direct consequence of the program or service rendered.

B. "What We Mean"

From these primary ideas, the teams then develop a brief explication of the meaning of their ideas of impact. This translates ideas that are occasionally technical into messages accessible to all.

C. Quantitative Indicators (E3)

Teams then identify quantitative indicators for each of the ideas. The aim is to generate five or six of the most critical indicators for each idea, paying attention to the data power, proxy power, and communication power of each of the key ideas. The intent in this step is to identify a range of cognitive, affective, and behavioral indicators that can be measured through metrics.

D Qualitative Indicators (E4)

Teams also identify qualitative indicators in this stage. These indicators are articulations of the structural and qualitative elements of growth and development that signal progress toward key ideas of impact. The qualitative indicators become the basis for the protocol construction to inform the in-depth interviews in the inquiry phase.

Part 2 - Inquiry

In the inquiry stage of the project, each team designs and implements a strategy for data gathering. These take two forms: a questionnaire to collect quantitative data and an in-depth interview to gather qualitative data.

A. Quantitative Data and Analysis

For each of the E3 indicators, teams construct items for a questionnaire. Since these projects are not intended to provide experimental or quasi-experimental inquiry, the attribution of effect is built into the questionnaire items. The questionnaire is deployed, in most cases, to the entire population of recipients the program reaches. Data are analyzed mostly using measures of central tendency. The teams then design displays of the data and narrative for their report.

B. Qualitative Data and Analysis

The development of a qualitative design encompasses a number of steps, including the following:

1. **Protocol Design.** Each team designs an in-depth interview protocol that uses the *Heart Triangle*™ method of question design. These produces a protocol of about nine sequences of questions (18 questions in total) to be used as a guide for seeking data about the awareness and reflection of subjects' structural shifts and developments of growth and progress.
2. **Sample.** Each team determines a sample of subjects using a purposeful stratified technique to identify a selection representative of the population being served.
3. **Data Collection.** Interviews are convened, most lasting between 45 minutes and 1 hour in length. Data are collected via notes during the interview, and then augmented immediately following the interview to provide a substantive rendering of the interview.
4. **Data Analysis.** Team members apply a four-step model of analysis to each of the interviews. This process provides them with a casual version of coding and interpretation, illuminating the primary themes from each interview.
5. **Thematics.** Through a guided and facilitative process, the entire data corpus is then examined. Themes are mapped through meta-analysis of the emerging insights.

3. Implication

The intent of the project is not to leave teams simply with a report about their program's effects, but rather to use the insights from the evaluation to guide the further development of the program. This takes two forms:

A. Program Adjustments

The team then takes each of the findings from the evaluation and considers possible program adjustments informed by the discoveries of the evaluation. This keeps the evaluation relevant for program application and improvement.

B. Program Experiments

In addition, the teams work to identify potential design experiments that they might run as an implication of the insights gained through the evaluation.

In this stage, the teams also begin to develop a report of the evaluation findings as well as other possible communiques of their discoveries to staff, stakeholders, funders, and other members of the community.

Explanation of the Reports

The reports from the organizations in this cohort are included in the following compendium. These include highlights from the three movements of the Project Impact. For each participating organization, there is an explication of the primary findings from the evaluation accompanied by the programmatic responses of strategy and design. Since each organization has unique strategy and ethos, each report exhibits unique character and personality. Each report also includes both "prove" findings (evidence of impacts being achieved) and "improve" findings (areas for attention and further development). These reports are windows into the effects of the work of these organizations in the lives of the people they serve.

PeopleShores

Aparna Gole

Introduction

PeopleShores is a technology and business process outsourcing enterprise with a charter to transform Opportunity Youth into knowledge professionals. Opportunity Youth are young adults who are disconnected from the education and employment systems and are often characterized by problems of poverty, lack of a supportive family system and inadequacy of social skills. Despite these problems, many of them are highly self-motivated and possess enormous untapped talent. They seek a chance to transcend past their barriers and seize opportunities that can put them on a track to success. The intentional hiring strategy of PeopleShores qualifies it as a pure-pay Impact Sourcing Services Provider[1].

Incorporated as a Public Benefit Corporation (PBC) in August 2017, PeopleShores' intent is to empower the talented young adults by

---

1   Impact Sourcing Services Providers are organizations within the Business Process Outsourcing (BPO) industry which typically have a mission to generate employment for and upgrade the skills of workers from poor and vulnerable communities. The procurement strategy or talent sourcing initiative of mainstream companies to hire employees from a disadvantaged population, be it themselves or through contracting work to an independent ISSP is called Impact Sourcing.

training them across various technology domains including Python, SQL, Adobe Premiere Pro, Google Analytics, Advanced Excel, Robotic Process Automation etc. while also providing them with other supporting workplace skills such as communication, interpersonal dynamics, discipline, and professionalism. Upon completion of the in-house training, the young adults are offered full-time employment at PeopleShores with full benefits including health insurance and paid leave. They are assigned to various processes /projects that are outsourced to PeopleShores by its customer organizations.

PeopleShores identifies its potential employees through an array of social service agencies that provide stability support to a section of the impacted youth through their programs. While the skills development and full-time employment at PeopleShores enables the young adults to gain financial freedom, self-confidence, and self-esteem, the community partners continue to provide the necessary counseling and stability support till they can stand on their own.

PeopleShores is a technology and business process outsourcing enterprise with a charter to transform Opportunity Youth into knowledge professionals. Opportunity Youth are young adults who are disconnected from the education and employment systems and are often characterized with problems of poverty, lack of a supportive family system and inadequacy of PeopleShores is a technology and business process outsourcing enterprise with a charter to transform Opportunity Youth into knowledge professionals.

Opportunity Youth are young adults who are disconnected from the education and employment systems and are often characterized by problems of poverty, lack of a supportive family system and inadequacy of social skills. Despite these problems, many of them are highly self-motivated and possess enormous untapped talent. They seek a chance to transcend past their barriers and seize opportunities that can put them on a track to success. The intentional hiring strategy of PeopleShores qualifies it as a pure-pay Impact Sourcing Services Provider.

Incorporated as a Public Benefit Corporation (PBC) in August 2017, PeopleShores' intent is to empower the talented young adults by training them across various technology domains including Python, SQL, Adobe premiere Pro, Google Analytics, Advanced Excel, Robotic Process Automation etc. while also providing them with other supporting workplace skills such as communication, interpersonal dynamics, discipline, and professionalism. Upon completion of the in-house training, the young adults are offered full-time employment at PeopleShores with full benefits including health insurance and paid leave. They are assigned to various processes /projects that are outsourced to PeopleShores by its customer organizations.

PeopleShores identifies its potential employees through an array of social service agencies that provide stability support to a section of the impacted youth through their own programs. While the skills development and fulltime employment at PeopleShores enables the young adults gain financial freedom, self-confidence and self-esteem, the community partners continue to provide the necessary counseling and stability support till they can stand on their own.

Currently, PeopleShores operates out of its first center in San Jose. A select few community partners who help with the hiring process as well as with provision of post hiring stability support (housing, childcare, legal assistance, emotional guidance etc.) are mentioned below:

At the time of publication of this report, PeopleShores had ~20 full-time employees and 6 members on the Leadership team. The full-time employees have in the past been characterized as home-less, victims of domestic violence, refugees, person with physical disability, or person on the autistic spectrum. These adjectives do not define the whole person that PeopleShores employees are, for they are much more than that. Beyond these incidental adjectives, PeopleShores employees are committed and motivated individuals yearning for a progressive career path in the hi-Tech industry and PeopleShores provides them that opportunity.

Intended Impacts

PeopleShores' intended impact for its employees is that having transcended the past barriers and seized the opportunities, our employees become successful corporate leaders and active social citizens. The Impact Statement is broken down into four key direct impacts. These are the effects PeopleShores can and would like to achieve at the core of its work:

➢ **Employees are financially secure and have an overall sense of personal well-being.**

Employees are given skills-training and a full-time job with a living wage to help them find their footing, get a sense of financial independence and start their journey on a progressive career opportunity.

➢ **Employees are on a progressive career path.**

While acquiring specific technical career-skills, employees also develop in-depth domain knowledge, demonstrate commitment and discipline to deliver on their responsibilities, develop a sense of ambition to progress to higher designations /show leadership tendencies, take initiative and showcase a sense of ownership and agency.

➢ **Employees are better able to deal with uncertainty and trauma.**

Employees feel supported by the available support structure at PeopleShores (designated caseworker or access to leadership team), enabling them to deal with uncertainty or challenges better, employees feel more in control of their emotions and develop a feeling of family or camaraderie.

➢ **Employees have developed a values-centric mindset.**

Employees follow role models, imbibe core human values (integrity, honesty, being righteous, sharing and caring for all), adhere to PeopleShores corporate values, show gratefulness for those underprivileged, and nurture service-orientation.

Evaluation Methodology

Our evaluation aimed to understand the impact PeopleShores is having on its employees. To understand this, we explored two broad research questions:

- ➤ What kind and quality of impact are we having on our employees?
- ➤ What aspects of our programming are causing this impact?

Over the course of the project, we (a) developed and refined our ideas of intended impact and indicators, (b) designed and implemented a mixed methods outcome evaluation using both qualitative and quantitative means to collect and analyze data, (c) identified findings, and (d) considered the implications to those findings for program improvement and innovation.

This project began with a focus on the work of identifying and clarifying the intended impact of PeopleShores. Once the ideas of impact had been developed, we used the Heart Triangle™ model to identify qualitative and quantitative indicators of impact focused on the mental, behavioral and emotional changes in our employees that indicate we are achieving our impact. We then used these indicators to design a qualitative interview protocol and a quantitative questionnaire to measure our progress toward achieving our intended impact.

Qualitative Data Collection and Analysis

For the qualitative portion of the evaluation, we designed an in-depth interview protocol to gain data about the structural, qualitative changes in employees resulting from their experience with PeopleShores. We used a purposeful stratified sampling technique to select a representative sample from the population we serve. Our population size was 18 employees. Our sample size was seven employees, and we drew our sample from the following strata of our population (one employee was counted in two categories):

- On autistic spectrum: 2
- Refugee: 1
- Suffered domestic violence: 2
- Homeless: 2
- Disabled: 1
- Gender: 5 male, 2 female
- Employee status: 4 staffed on client projects, 3 still in training

We then convened one-on-one interviews lasting from between 45 minutes and one hour in length with the sample of employees. Interviewers took notes during the interviews and filled in the notes immediately after the interview to obtain a substantive rendering of the interview.

We analyzed the qualitative interview data inductively using a modified version of thematic analysis. The interviewer implemented the first three phases of thematic analysis (becoming familiar with the data, generating initial codes and identifying themes) for each interview. The interviewer familiarized herself with the data by reviewing the data from each interview four times, each time thinking through a different aspect of what the data reveal about the research questions. The interviewer then assigned the data into four categories to serve as an initial set of codes. Finally, the interviewer generated initial themes based on the pervasive insights from the data. This process allowed us to interpret the meaning and significance of the data from each interview.

Next, we brought all of the data analyses and initial themes together and implemented the next two phases of thematic analysis (reviewing themes, defining and naming themes). We reviewed the initial themes to identify the overarching themes that emerged from the full scope of our data analysis to illuminate the collective insights and discoveries. We mapped these themes visually and examined them in various ways to gain greater definition of the features of the themes, the causes and catalysts of the themes, new or surprising insights related to the themes, and the relationships between the themes that were revealed in the data. We then determined the most significant and meaningful discoveries and brought them forward as findings to be described in the final phase of thematic analysis, this report.

Quantitative Data and Analysis

For the quantitative portion of the evaluation, we designed a questionnaire to collect data on our quantitative indicators of impact. The survey instrument consisted of multiple-choice questions, retrospective Likert-scale response, as well as a few open-ended short answer questions. We administered this instrument to all 18 employees and received a response from each employee for a 100% response rate. The data were analyzed primarily using measures of central tendency. We identified key insights, patterns, and gaps within the data and incorporated these discoveries into the related findings.

Findings
Finding #1: Personality 2.0

Description

PeopleShores' raison d'etre is to provide opportunities for its employees for learning new concepts and skills which will help them progress their careers in the technology industry. While undergoing the training, is how the journey of a typical PeopleShores employee starts, the real test comes when an employee is asked to deploy that learning in a client context, which requires him/her to have:

> ➢ Core technical skills: coding in SQL or Python; mastery over Adobe Premier Pro or other creative suite of products, Google Analytics, Robotic Process Automation, etc.
> ➢ Allied personality skills
> • Confidence

- Discipline
- Leadership
- Time management and organization
- Tenacity or ability to overcome difficulty

In addition to the key skills that are 'intentional skill-development of employees' and is part of PeopleShores' strategic intent, employees also go through personal transformation (which might loop back into how their two core skill areas develop as well). These could be socio-dynamic facets of one's personality and typically may include

➢ Perception of self against peers

➢ Awareness of one's potential

➢ Developing a sense of emotional equilibrium

During the evaluation exercise, the evaluation team thus was keen to understand who PeopleShores employees have become (having spent some time within PeopleShores), how they have changed and to what extent are those changes attributable to they being in PeopleShores. A series of interview questions as well as survey questions have helped get an insight into those questions, and the same are discussed in this finding henceforth.

PeopleShores is only about nine months old at the time of publishing this report, and most of its employees have been put through a variety of training courses over this period. The evaluation team was keen to understand how the employees perceived the training regarding its overall utility for employees' professional future. Employees were asked via the survey instrument to what extent the skills they have learned at PeopleShores have helped them grow professionally; to which nearly 50% of the employees responded positively ('very much' or 'a lot' response).

see chart on next page

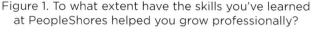

Figure 1. To what extent have the skills you've learned at PeopleShores helped you grow professionally?

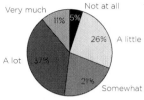

It needs to be additionally noted that at the time of publication of this report, only a proportion of PeopleShores employees are working on client projects, but almost all are working on simulated client situations to adapt the classroom learning into a real-life situation; so, it would be safe to say that only a few employees know how the learning at PeopleShores translates into client work in reality, while many employees have some finite level of understanding of the same. Romeo shared, "We have learned many things in PeopleShores. Right from coding, to mortgage processing, to insurance claim generation, to even image processing and Microsoft excel!" He added, "As I work at a client site, I realize that I more flexible about the work I do."

During the interviews, it also came to the fore that employees have improved confidence, they are starting to be more disciplined, they are more analytical and that they are getting more organized as well as resourceful. Many of them also shared that they have developed tenacity or ability to overcome difficulty (this being an important finding, is explored separately ahead in this report). One employee described, "One of my friends said that in the couple of months she has known me, I have changed. I am growing in [a] way that I have better knowledge of how to interact with people. I know how to stay 'in-tact.' She (my friend) also said that I am more analytical than I was before!"

They went on to add, "Some of these things have helped me change in other areas too; I now know who looks less busy on a VTA platform and might be interested in helping me find directions; of course, I am getting better at reading maps too!" Another reflected, "I have learned how to find answers quickly and efficiently. Like using keywords or close caption searches, scrubbing videos and so on. My commitment is the same, but the hindrances are now resolved more efficiently. I have become more resourceful." He shared, "I have learned how to find answers quickly and efficiently. Like using keywords or close caption searches, scrubbing videos and so on. My commitment is the same, but the hindrances are now resolved more efficiently. I have become more resourceful." Despite significant growth in a variety of professional skills, employee growth in leadership capability is lagging. Given that some of the PeopleShores employees have worked in the past, when asked about the change they perceived in themselves about their leadership capabilities, about 20% of employees (4) gave highly positive responses, while most (15) suggested moderate improvement in their leadership skills. The simple reason for the same could be that employees still do not understand what being in the position of leadership might mean, especially in the PeopleShores' context, and some might truly not feel that they are ready for the same. At the same time, through the interviews, there have been some expressed desires to become managers in the distant future. For instance, one participant claimed that he wishes to be a product manager.

Figure 2. I am more disciplined

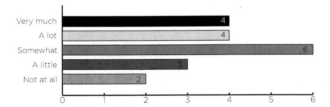

The significant professional growth in employees has positively changed the employees socio-dynamically as well. Among the most significant areas of personal growth are increased awareness of their potential and feeling of being equal with peers outside PeopleShores. One shared, "I am not overthinking and getting overwhelmed too easily. I feel a bit optimistic, comfortable, ready to embrace the idea of living a corporate life. Before [PeopleShores], I was too fearful of it, now, I am embracing it."

When employees were asked about 'feeling equal' to peers outside of PeopleShores, most employees believed that they felt 'somewhat equal.'

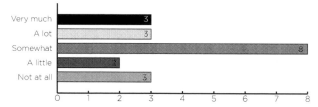

Figure 3. I feel more equal to peers outside PeopleShores

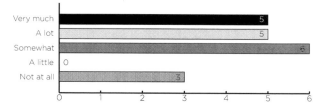

Figure 4. I am more aware of my own potential

Lastly, when asked about how employees feel emotionally before and after PeopleShores, the response was mixed, with not a significant proportion feeling 'completely' in control of their emotions; but almost 75% of employees feeling at least some level of control ('very much', 'a lot' and 'somewhat' responses).

Significance

It is clear that PeopleShores employees are becoming a new and better version of themselves with higher skills, confidence, discipline, time management abilities and control over emotional outbursts. For some of them, the baggage of the past seems to have reduced a bit, and the ability to feel equal to other non-disadvantaged youth seems like a definite possibility. This is an excellent observation for PeopleShores since this feedback confirms some of the strategies PeopleShores has implemented to train the candidates, to deploy them on client projects as well as to create a conducive atmosphere for them where they will feel loved, valued and respected

Many of the traits and skills learned while at PeopleShores seem to be helping shape employees' overall personalities outside of work, an important dynamic for those on the autistic spectrum, but equally important for others. While a happy-spillover is something that is not intentioned by PeopleShores, the feedback loop from the same might change the personalities of employees such that they may have a higher desire for learning, higher hunger for success and increased confidence. All of these are critical aspects to employees' professional success, be it at PeopleShores or otherwise.

Some employees do not feel entirely in control of their emotions, nor do they completely believe in their capabilities as a leader. While a part of that can be attributed to the fact that PeopleShores is a young organization with most of its employees in their first job, (and only a few of the employees being deployed on PeopleShores' client projects), some specific initiatives might be necessary to change this current dynamic.

Possible Responses

A few additional coaching sessions on the Friday Foresight Platform (an employee engagement initiative where guests outside of PeopleShores come and share their knowledge) might be necessary to help demystify how leadership in a hi-tech company looks like, what skills may be required for the leadership positions and what kind of person, temperamentally, is usually a good fit for being a leader.

Secondly, while PeopleShores has mostly relied on the stability support coming through designated caseworker (assigned by the agency that recommended the PeopleShores employee), some additional in-house expertise may need to get built that will help navigate the workplace challenges too. This could be a formal mentorship program or informal coaching or a check-in platform. As more and more employees start getting mapped on client projects, which will bring its own pressures and challenges, the need for coaching and mentorship will become more pronounced too.

Finding #2: Dreams > Difficulty

Description

A typical employee's career path at PeopleShores starts with rigorous training and post that working on client projects. As one develops specific skills that are required to perform a project task, one also develops the allied skills of time management, process or project management, client engagement, etc. naturally. PeopleShores will also start providing additional training for these allied traits in months to come, in line with clients' potential requirements, as well as employees' career interests.

During the interview process, most of the employees shared that they feel their Technology skills have either undergone a refresh or that they have started to build the same from scratch. Evaluation team often heard that this has mainly been made possible through rigorous training that PeopleShores employees are subjected to, but often with a possibility to learn at one's own pace. For some of the employees, who have had Tech experience in the past, this meant rebuilding of the skills and confidence to have a tech-oriented career, while for some other, it meant getting an understanding of how their inherent skills and interests peg against the requirements of a Tech job.

For some, who have worked in other sectors such as retail stores, the training and working opportunity at PeopleShores meant finding out the best way they can transition to a career in the Tech sector, having understood potential synergies from their past work experience. Whether learning the tech skills anew or undergoing a refresh, most employees felt positive about how the future career might unfold for them, which is evidenced from the fact that three-fourths of them said to have greater dreams for their future.

Figure 5. I have greater dreams for my future

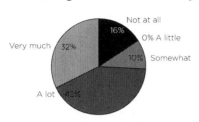

One employee, who had worked in the Tech sector in the past, said, "It [training and experience at PeopleShores] has given me hope that I have it in me to go back to the Tech sector." Another who did not have a background in Tech, said, "I think my future prospects have improved greatly. Doors I did not think would open or even existed, now seem like a possibility; it's like I have a key in my pocket!"

One employee shared, "Before I came to PeopleShores, I was trying to shape my thinking about my future career. But it was not organized and was very vague. I was not clear [about] what I was going to do. I was changing my career to hi-tech, and I was wondering how I will handle this change. But at PeopleShores, I learned how to make this change happen in an organized manner. I am learning what to focus on and what skills I may need for the future." When employees were probed further during the quantitative survey to find out ways in which their situation has changed after joining PeopleShores, which might have been the reason to feel better about their future, interesting findings emerged.

Firstly, almost 50% employees believed that their 'personal situation' had improved significantly ('a lot' or 'very much' responses) since joining PeopleShores, which can be explained by a simple fact that all the employees get a living wage and benefits. Secondly, many felt that they may now get a chance to further their education. Some found that PeopleShores is a great segue to the bigger career dreams they have.

Needless to say, the skills employees are building have also improved how they perceive their ability to complete future project tasks and client assignments with an emphatic 75% of employees claiming that they feel confident of meeting all the project goals within the stipulated time with the experience they are gaining at PeopleShores ('frequently' and 'very frequently' responses).

When employees were asked about how the confidence emanating from the skills and experience at PeopleShores shapes their thinking about their future, about half the employees, felt that they would be ready for a leadership position (team lead, process lead, etc.) over next 3-5 years. Interestingly, some of the employees talked about their realization that coding is not interesting to them and that they have started to think about developing technical skills (such as process automation or bot maintenance) that may help them with their career. For instance, one employee talked about his desire to master Adobe's creative suite of products and get certified. Another said that he realized early on that he may not be a coder, but this realization is making him look at other technical, non-coding opportunities and skills closely. In general, it was PeopleShores' finding that the employees had come to believe that they are on a career path that is progressive and that they are not merely doing a job anymore.

Significance

At an overall level, most PeopleShores employees showcased positivity and optimism about their professional career. Given the fact that whether in training, on the bench or a client project, upon completion of the probation, employees of PeopleShores get paid a living wage, get leave credit and also benefits, makes them feel less stressed financially. To not have the employees feel financially stressed was a core intention of PeopleShores leadership team. By design, PeopleShores carries the burden of risk to make each employee successful, once the employee is part of the PeopleShores team. This is unlike many other coding, training nonprofits that might train a candidate in their program but may not provide the candidate with full-time employment at the end of the training. The fact that employees showcase less stress, thus confirms PeopleShores' operational hypothesis.

Between the findings 1 and 2, it was evident that not all employees feel ready to be leaders right away, but many employees do feel that they would like to be leaders in 3-5 years; this requires some further understanding and deep-dive. If the employees are ambitious and want to be leaders (which is what PeopleShores would want them to achieve too, in the long term), some strategic initiatives might be necessary for the immediate future

Almost a quarter of the employees would like to further their education, something which is not surprising given that many of the PeopleShores employees have only a high-school diploma and not a college degree at the time of joining PeopleShores. There might be an opportunity for PeopleShores to work with local community colleges to get course credits and to find ways to enable PeopleShores employees to get their degrees or diploma certificates.

Possible Responses

While a standard training and career progression plan exist for employees of PeopleShores; given the bigger dreams employees have for their future (especially with some employees having definite role and designation in their minds), the time might be right to encapsulate an individualized yet scalable 'career development plan' for PeopleShores' future needs. Given the need for furthering education, but also being cognizant of potential economic job loss with Artificial Intelligence, Machine Learning, and Robotic Process Automation becoming part of everyday reality, PeopleShores could consider partnering with local community colleges to identify and/or develop courses where PeopleShores clients might foresee additional demand.

Figure 6. To what extent does PeopleShores make you
feel more supported than you felt before PeopleShores,
in your moments of difficulty?

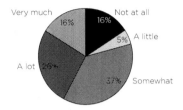

Finding #3: La Mia Famiglia!

Description

Most of PeopleShores employees have either not had a sense of family (and thereby the stability families bring in one's life) or have lost it during their lifetimes. During the interview process, it became evident that almost all the respondents think that through PeopleShores, they are increasingly building a sense of belonging and a sense of camaraderie. They are also able to find a place of solace and a channel to confide in.

In parallel, employees also increasingly feel that their cultural horizons are broadening through PeopleShores: be it food being shared during lunch hours or different holidays and birthdays being celebrated, all of which contribute to the family-like atmosphere. One employee observed, "They [PeopleShores founder and Leadership Team] try to understand our situation, and they try to give us support. And they tell us to ask if we need any help. I never felt like I should not say this or should not ask this. I feel like I am 'easy' here. Once you are in PeopleShores, you have different supports in different ways. This gives you better control on yourself. There is always motivation and encouragement here." Another shared, "I have never held a job before where different holidays were celebrated!"

An additional and important aspect of the support system at PeopleShores that employees found particularly helpful was the presence of a caseworker. Many interviewees mentioned the caseworker specifically and discussed the importance of knowing there is someone they can turn to in times of need. As many as 80% of employees said that they felt supported in moments of difficulty, at least to some extent. Employees also valued that the caseworker was available to regularly check in on them and proactively see how they're doing before a problem becomes too big. One reflected, "It definitely helps that there is a caseworker. A caseworker being able to come to just poke her head through and ask if you need help means a lot. I know, if anyone needs any help, or has any questions, the caseworkers will be willing to help." Another observed, "the career counselor I was assigned to truly helped me find alignment from my skillsets and past work-experience and apply the same anew."

Having the family-like support system has helped employees overcome challenges that seemed daunting to them before. For instance, employees shared how they are now able to work through miscommunication better, have figured out how not to leave things unresolved, and how to work through diverse personalities and differences of opinions. While this is truer for the employees who happen to be on the autistic spectrum, it is also true for most others as noted here, "Support system is very important, and it helps. I can now always think of someone to talk to and get a suggestion from. Maybe this person will not have a solution, but even suggestion from them would help." At an overall level, this supportive feeling has resulted in almost 90% of employees, feeling quite happy to be at PeopleShores.

Significance

The fact that most PeopleShores employees are increasingly building a sense of family and camaraderie and are finding a place to confide in is an excellent testament of PeopleShores thinking correctly about its employee engagement initiatives as well as its overall business model. While not a significant proportion of employees feel entirely emotionally supported, almost all said that they are happy to be at PeopleShores. A part of this can be attributed to the fact that most of the employees are still building trust. For an employee who joined on day 1, it has been nine months knowing PeopleShores, but for many others, the association is less than six months old!

An additional potential reason for all the employees not feeling fully supported could also be because there is no formal in-house channel at PeopleShores that employees can tap into. Most employees who feel supported tend to reach out to the leadership team or their colleagues on their own, but some others might need a more formal and more confidential channel to work through their workplace difficulties.

Possible Responses

Some additional investigation might be needed into seeing, outside of the case-worker given stability support, what more can PeopleShores do to help all of its employees feel emotionally supported. For instance, there might be a need to have an entirely devoted case worker designated for each PeopleShores center who is available as 'on-site, on-call stability support.' PeopleShores could create an employee engagement calendar that can keep employees motivated and engaged with some visibility on future family-style events. This will not only help strengthen the current friendly atmosphere but also give a more informal channel for employees to work through their workplace hiccups and create additional bonds of friendship.

Finding #4: Commit to 'Meet the Goals'

Description

During the interview process, it became apparent that employees have started realizing the importance of hard work, have started giving their best to achieve project deadlines and personal goals alike, and have started finding ways to overcome the impediments standing in the way of achieving those. More than 60% of employees said that they feel highly committed ('very much' or 'a lot') to overcoming difficulties standing in the way of their goals. As one participant noted, "Before [PeopleShores], my commitment was very loose. I would work half time and not the rest of the time. But here at PeopleShores, I am 100% committed. I have stayed back late to get the project finished on more than one occasion."

Figure 7. I am more committed to overcome difficulties standing in the way of my goals

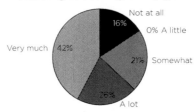

As one woman described, "I try to think of life's curveballs - I sit back and say, 'that it is just a curveball'! I stand up back on my feet. I just say that there was something to be learned there and let's now move on to learning something else. Before PeopleShores, everything was going downhill. But by being here, I knew things have started going up a little, and the pace at which they are going up is high." Another employee shared that he did not even know how the clock gets to 5:30 pm, (end of the business day at PeopleShores), to indicate that training and working at PeopleShores is that enjoyable! Other added that having idle time at work is at times more difficult than being busy training or working on projects!

Employees have also begun to realize that in order to achieve their goals, they will at times, have to take the team along, which will necessitate having cordial relationships with those on the team. An employee talked about how he worked through personal differences of those on his team to get a task completed, and how he is now increasingly focusing on keeping 'clean air' with his colleagues. This was echoed by another participant, "I am not on a project that is to my absolute liking. But I am willing to excel at it, work with my project manager, and find ways to get onto a project that will be to my absolute liking."

Some of the tenacity and commitment PeopleShores employees are developing have also started to color employees' personal lives. Romeo, who happens to be on autistic spectrum said, "I am becoming more committed to grow and improve myself. Be more flexible. Prove that I am a jack of all trades. That I can get along with everyone." To some extent, employees also claim that they can confront and overcome the problems, and not avoid them like an ostrich. For instance, some of them shared how they are able to look at the bigger picture, respect personal differences, and work through the difficulties to achieve the overall good.

Significance

More than 60% of employees claiming that they feel highly committed to overcoming difficulties standing in the way of their goals is a great solace for PeopleShores for two reasons: (a) commitment cannot be bought in the market or taught in a classroom (b) most of PeopleShores employees are dealing with a life-difficulty and the ability to stay committed despite that, is a great feature to being successful at PeopleShores, be it while training or while working on the assigned client project.

Another happy outcome to persevering through difficulty is also being able to encounter the problems upfront (or head-on) and finding ways to overcome those, all while not hampering the workplace culture. Most of the PeopleShores employees are able to achieve many of these softer traits through the way their personalities are getting shaped, and at times, there is also a happy spillover of these traits in employees' personal lives.

Possible Responses

In months to come, as PeopleShores starts securing more client work, there might be a need to start thinking of a more formal channel for workplace issue resolution. For large client-focused teams, this could be in the form of a designated, all-hands meeting, while for all other employees (who are in training or on the bench), it can be a formal monthly check-in with the designated mentor / HR personnel. This will ensure that employees do not have to persevere through the workplace difficulties in agony, and will have a formal mechanism to seek resolution.

Finding #5: Instilling the Ideals

Description

The leadership of PeopleShores tries to expose the employees to value-centric behavior through their own actions, by hosting sessions specifically on the topic (via employee engagement platforms such as Friday foresight). In addition, it seeks to actively encourage workplace behavior that is in accordance with core employee values of teamwork, working through social and cultural differences, openness, honesty, humility and so on.

During the interview process, it was apparent that the employees have started embracing and practicing many of the positive workplace ideals and virtues. The ideals that were most cited as learned during interviews were inclusion and acceptance of social, personal and cultural diversity, conflict resolution through mutual respect and understanding, openness, honesty (yet having your say where due!), listening and supporting each other. Via the quantitative survey instrument, when employees were asked 'What two PeopleShores values are most meaningful to you?', 'teamwork' stood out quite boldly!

Figure 8. How much more meaningful are Corporate Giving or Corporate Service activities to you now, than they were before you were a part of PeopleShores?

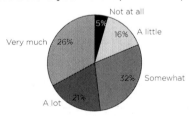

Employees claimed that practicing these values has helped them get back in touch with themselves and their innate goodness, widened their horizons, improved their interpersonal skills and helped them achieve more, and feel happier. One described, "I feel myself growing more mature. It's like the frog in boiling water. If you put a frog in boiling water it will jump out, but not if the water warms slowly. So, the changes I am undergoing might not seem like they are happening, but they are there. And I might find myself in a different place in life!" Yet another shared, "Now I am less likely to pounce and end in a confrontation. I am trying to see where they [people with a contrarian view] might be coming from." And further, "At PeopleShores, I am reminded of how big of a heart I had and how much I care about others. With my knee injury and derailed study plans, I was off to a downward spiral. But since coming to PeopleShores, I am getting some of that back. People talk to me an earful of their problems sometimes, and I am happy to be there to listen to them!"

Incidentally, two of the seven interviewees claimed to have 'dropped their friends', which surprised the evaluation team a great deal and caused the need for further understanding of what that might mean. One employee shared, "Actually, I just dropped most of my friends. Not all of them! (smiles). I do not hang out much. I realize who is really there and who is not. So, I just keep my circle small - private life is a happier life! I think I can read people a little bit better now." Another said, "My friends challenged me about why I am not like before. They started leaving me. But I am using my time effectively. And I am spending more time here [at PeopleShores], I do not want to be like before." On closer examination of data and body language of employees, it was apparent that as the employees of PeopleShores are moving towards being more disciplined and committed to work, they are letting go of friends who stand in the way of that.

Alongside instilling the ideals, employees of PeopleShores have also engaged in corporate giving activities like serving the homeless with warm food, sorting and bagging food at a local food bank over the last nine months. Given that PeopleShores would like its employees to go beyond the workplace values of Teamwork, Honesty, Acceptance of differences, etc. and embrace the importance of corporate giving and service activities, it was a consolation to see about half of PeopleShores employees finding these service activities meaningful.

Additionally, when this data is mapped against the fact that many of the PeopleShores employees themselves are currently dealing with some difficulty in life, the proportion of support for corporate giving does look encouraging. Additionally, there have been some further indications that employees continue to stay in touch with people living in difficulty (for instance, Murphy shared that he has routine conversations with the homeless) and have realizations of how fortunate they are to have found PeopleShores (with almost all the interviewed employees expressing gratefulness for working at PeopleShores, a question that was not specifically asked to them). In summary, PeopleShores employees seem to be progressing well towards becoming value-centric individuals.

Significance

One would agree that most people cannot carry two different personas: one for work and one in personal life (for it might be a great burden). It is thus, not surprising that PeopleShores employees are not only imbibing the values that they are exposed to at work but also are carrying the same over in their personal lives. Dropping non-committal friends being one such example. From PeopleShores' point of view, this carry-over is quite significant because, in a distant future, PeopleShores would like to see value-centric behavior of its employees spread to the professional teams they become part of, and in parallel influence their own families.

For many of the PeopleShores employees whose first job happens to be at PeopleShores, the cultural and social horizon thus far has been quite narrow. Added with the fact that there is emphatic racial, social, religious and cultural diversity at PeopleShores or in San

Francisco Bay Area, most employees feel that they have developed a greater understanding of differences that surround them and a have a higher acceptance for the same.

PeopleShores employees are valuing corporate giving, and corporate service is critically important for PeopleShores, given that its intended impact is not just to create Corporate leaders, but also to create active social citizen. So, while the current proportion of employees supporting social causes is encouraging, it would be great to have a significantly high proportion of employees show support for corporate giving. Lastly, if one were to peg the PeopleShores employee population of 19 against the order of the magnitude of ~13K disconnected youth in Santa Clara or ~4.6M in the US, it is imperative that each PeopleShores employee becomes the channel to further PeopleShores mission in years to come. Becoming a value-driven person is therefore very important in PeopleShores' context.

Possible Responses:
There might be a need for PeopleShores to continue to create awareness of the social and economic problems that it is surrounded by. While PeopleShores itself is a social enterprise, and while many of its employees might be dealing with a life-difficulty, there might be an opportunity to create a formal corporate giving program. At its inception, the program could be a simpler format and have only a few strategies such as (a) 1 day of service/year or (b) $10 employee matching program at year end or (c) volunteer Saturday at a local nonprofit that requires physical labor. Based on the response received in months and years to come, the program features can be additionally enhanced.

Conclusion and Next Steps
Based on the findings from the evaluation exercise and having identified the significance of each of those in the PeopleShores context, several key action items emerged (as covered above under

each of the findings). Following graphical representation gives a broad implementation plan to put into action some of those action items.

Over the Next 3 Months:
- ➤ Create an employee engagement calendar for future family-style events
- ➤ Launch a formal channel for workplace issue resolution
- ➤ Conduct a few additional coaching session on Friday Foresight Platform to demystify leadership in the hi-tech industry
- ➤ Start planning and ideation for launching "individual career development plan."

Over the Next Year:
- ➤ Build addition in-house expertise on providing 'on-site, on-call stability support
- ➤ Develop and launch a coaching/mentorship program
- ➤ Start conversations with local community colleges to identify and/or develop courses where PeopleShores' clients might see additional demand
- ➤ Start creating awareness about the social and economic problems in Silicon Valley and beyond
- ➤ Start planning for a formal corporate giving program

Next 1-3 Years:
- ➤ Launch a formal corporate giving program
- ➤ Continue creating awareness about the social and economic problems in Silicon Valley and beyond
- ➤ Formalize partnerships with local community colleges

Ronald McDonald House Charities of Southern California

Camp Ronald McDonald for Good Times

Fatima Djelmane, Shannon Edwards
Chad Edwards, Marlene Stang

Introduction to Ronald McDonald House Charities of Southern California

In 1980, RMHCSC opened the region's first Ronald McDonald House near Children's Hospital Los Angeles, followed by the start of Camp Ronald McDonald for Good Times in 1982. Over the next 35 years, RMHCSC opened six more Ronald McDonald Houses near major pediatric hospitals across the region. Today, RMHCSC houses have a total of 175 guest rooms that serve more than 17,000 family members every year; RMHCSC Camp is nationally recognized for its year-round, residential oncology camp programs.

Throughout the world, the Ronald McDonald House Charities partner with local hospitals serving critically ill children to strengthen community approaches to family-centered care. Our Houses and Family Rooms allow parents to remain close to their children during hospital stays, have a space to rest and care for themselves, and connect with other families that face similar challenges and fears. All of this ensures that parents are in a healthier frame of mind when it comes time to make decisions about their child's care.

In Southern California, we have deepened our approach to enhancing family-centered care through our camp program, Camp Ronald McDonald for Good Times. "Camp" functions year-round and was designed to help children build their self-esteem, self-reliance and independence after experiencing cancer.

Camp Ronald McDonald for Good Times:
"Where Healing Happens"
Camp Ronald McDonald for Good Times ("Camp") is the only year-round camp focused on the needs of children with cancer and their families in Southern California. For over thirty-five years, Camp has been on the forefront of designing medically supervised programs that respond to the needs of the pediatric oncology community. Today, we are one of the world's largest oncology camp programs, serving over 1,600 campers every year from all over our region with fun-filled, medically supervised, cost-free camp programs. We also host the first Spanish language camps in the nation to support our Southern California based Latino families impacted by childhood cancer.

All of our programs are offered at our 60 acre facility in Mountain Center near Idyllwild, which is comprised of 14 cabins (200 beds), a pool, activity areas, hiking trails, a multi-use dining hall and meeting space, Ed Rasky Archery Range, Jackson Fishing Pond and a "Med Shed." The "Med Shed" is our comprehensive Health Care Center, where all of our campers' medical needs are attended to 24/7 while at camp. We are in the midst of finalizing plans for a new cabin village, as well as a new amphitheater for performances and various activities.

Family Camp (which is the focus of our Project Impact interviews and evaluation) is offered to families of children with cancer ages 0-8. Families with children older than 8 years of age who are considering Summer Camp are also encouraged to attend Family Camp so they can familiarize themselves with the site, staff and program. Six Family Camp sessions are conducted in English and two are conducted in Spanish. The weekend- long camp is designed to be fun and supportive for all members of the family. Parents and children engage in activities that encourage teambuilding and bonding. Families form new bonds, find new support systems and build friendships and relationships that last during their child's treatment and beyond. Whether a child has an amputated leg, is using a wheelchair or walker, or has compromised vision, staff and volunteers are trained to ensure everyone can participate in camp programming. Activities at Family Camp include: archery, basketball, soccer, hiking, fishing, arts & crafts, nature exploration, music/dance, and more. The goal of our Family Camp program is to create a sense of community and belonging among families living with childhood cancer.

As a result of attending Family Camp, we intend to impact families in the following ways:

1. **Families reconnect and reestablish a sense of normalcy.** Family Camp allows families to get away for a weekend for what's serves for many as the only vacation they take each year. Families have time to relax, rebuild and strengthen family bonds. They are provided opportunities to return to a sense of normalcy – play, laugh, eat meals, and talk together again – to participate in everyday activities that were put on hold during treatment.

2. **Families build relationships and support networks with other families.** Family Camp allows families to meet other families going through the cancer journey – some on the same road, some where they once were, and some where they hope to be one day. Families connect with one another, build long-lasting friendships, and develop relationships that serve as peer support networks they lean on after Camp is over.

3. **Families are informed and empowered to move forward in their cancer journey.** Family Camp allows families the opportunity to be part of a safe and supportive environment where questions and conversations are welcomed. Volunteer counselors facilitate safe and engaging activities where kids

are allowed to be kids again, and where parents can see first-hand the benefit of Camp in the lives of their children. Parents are given the time to meet with other parents and staff to ask advice, share resources, or express successes and challenges around their cancer journey.

Evaluation Methodology

The aim of our evaluation was to see what kind and quality of impact Family Camp is having on the families that attend. To understand this, we explored two broad research questions:

1. What kind and quality of impact are we having on families with children facing cancer?
2. What aspects of our program are causing this impact?

Over the course of the project, we (a) developed and refined our ideas of intended impact and indicators, (b) designed and implemented a mixed methods outcome evaluation using both qualitative and quantitative means to collect and analyze data, (c) identified findings, and (d) considered the implications to those findings for program improvement and innovation.

This project began with a focus on the work of identifying and clarifying the intended impact of Family Camp. Once the ideas of impact had been developed, we used the Heart Triangle™ model to identify qualitative and quantitative indicators of impact focused on the mental, behavioral and emotional changes families experience that indicate we are achieving our impact. We then used these indicators to design a qualitative interview protocol and a quantitative questionnaire to measure our progress toward achieving our intended impact.

Qualitative Data Collection and Analysis

For the qualitative portion of the evaluation, we designed an in-depth interview protocol to gain data about the structural, qualitative changes resulting from our program. We used a purposeful stratified sampling technique to select a representative sample from the population we serve. Our population size was 121. Our sample size was 12 and we drew our sample from the following strata of our population:

> ➤ Families who attended Family Camp in 2018
> ➤ Families who attended Family Camp one or more time with the last two years

Our interview team consisted of Camp Ronald McDonald for Good Times' Executive Director Fatima Djelmane Rodriquez, Development Director Marlene Stang, Program Director Chadwick Edwards and Program Associate Shannon Edwards.

We then convened one-on-one interviews lasting from between 45 minutes and one hour in length with a sample from the identified strata of the population. Interviewers took notes during the interviews and filled in the notes immediately after the interview to obtain a substantive rendering of the interview.

We analyzed the data inductively using a modified version of thematic analysis. Interviewers implemented the first three phases of thematic analysis (becoming familiar with the data, generating initial codes and identifying themes) for each interview. The interviewers familiarized themselves with the data by reviewing the data from each interview four times, each time thinking through a different aspect of what the data reveal about the research question. The data were then bucketed into four categories to serve as an initial set of codes. Finally, initial themes were generated based on the pervasive insights from the data. This process allowed us to interpret the meaning and significance of the data from each interview.

Next, we brought all of the data analyses and initial themes together and implemented the next two phases of thematic analysis (reviewing themes, defining and naming themes). We reviewed the initial themes as a team to identify the overarching themes that emerged from the full scope of our data analysis to illuminate the collective insights and discoveries. We mapped these themes visually and examined them in various ways to gain greater definition of the features of the themes, causes and catalysts of the themes, new or surprising insights related to the themes, and relationships between the themes that were revealed in the data. We then determined the most significant and meaningful discoveries and brought them forward as findings to be described in the final phase of thematic analysis, this report.

Quantitative Data and Analysis

For the quantitative portion of the evaluation, we designed a questionnaire to collect data on our quantitative indicators of impact. We administered this instrument via Survey Monkey to 121 families that had attended Family Camp one or more times within the past 2 years and received a response from 21 families, a 17.35% response rate. The data were analyzed primarily using measures of central tendency. We identified key insights, patterns, and gaps within the data and incorporated these discoveries into the related findings.

The most significant discoveries from this evaluation are described in the findings that follow.

We narrowed our study to focusing on the impact of Family Camp for the families we serve. For the qualitative portion of the process, we interviewed a total of 12 families both in person and over the phone. We focused on families that have attended Camp at least twice to better assess Camp's impact over time. Interviews were conducted by Camp's Executive Director, Development Director, Program Director and Program Associate. Data from the survey has been folded into our findings from the qualitative interviews.

Findings

Finding 1: Game Changers

Key Insight: Camp Ronald McDonald for Good Times is a place where families first encounter other parents and volunteers who can share life-changing resources for their children and their families.

Description

The data reveal that for a lot of parents Family Camp is the first time they hear about resources to support their child and family. Being catapulted into the medical world is daunting for every family we spoke to and is especially overwhelming when they are also dealing with the emotional trauma of having a newly-diagnosed child. Even for families who have access to more resources and a formal education, the data showed that families were all exposed to new information and resources when they came to Family Camp.

When families were asked "What are the three most helpful new resources that you learned about at Camp?" on our quantitative survey, answers provided by our survey respondents ranged from the practical (i.e. "How to request a 'child life' worker at hospital in-patient visits.") to program-based resources like "Capes and Crowns" (a non-profit that provides one-of-a-kind fantasy photo ops to children with illnesses) and "The Sunshine Kids Foundation" (a non-profit that provides meaningful group activities and emotional support to children with cancer.)

In our interviews, many parents described a variety of resources they discovered through attending camp. One parent learned that Camp could connect her and her family to Family Support Services (FSS, a therapy program offered at the Ronald McDonald Houses), so now she's going to look into it utilizing this service. Another family also learned about the Ronald McDonald House Charities of Southern California Family Support Services through Camp and have told others about the benefits of the resource for them as parents and for their children. One parent shared, "The medical western health system is not taking a holistic approach to healing. They don't look at the whole body, just the diagnosis. The psychological ability to move on in the world is difficult, but FSS and Camp help alleviate that for us." For one of our parents, Family Camp was the first time they learned of resources to help with their son's struggles in school. They shared, "I heard about the 104 plan and IEP. I had no clue about all that before Family Camp. [Thanks to Camp], I was able to get [my son] more time. We just got a 104 plan set up, so that he can do better."

Significance

The data revealed that Camp is a valuable place where families learn new information and gain access to resources. This is significant because families may not receive information about resources for remission and survivorship from their medical providers, whose primary concern is treating disease. We also realize that families need ongoing support outside of Camp as well so that they can continue to be informed of and connected to more holistic resources. What this would look like (a bricks and mortar facility or online support network, for example) requires further discussion. The cancer journey does not end at remission, so resources and support are needed throughout the child's life.

Possible Responses

- ➤ Create an online forum for parents.
- ➤ Add a resource tab to our website.
- ➤ Provide families with a resource binder when they first join Camp.
- ➤ Include a resource corner in family newsletter that is distributed currently.
- ➤ Host quarterly family meetings at the RMHCSC houses as an additional touch point for parents.

Finding 2: Cancer Unites Us

Key Insight: Regardless of race, gender, sexual orientation, or socioeconomic status, our campers are able to find common ground in their cancer journeys.

Description

Interviewees across the board shared that Camp is a place where their children are able to leave their diagnosis at the door and just be themselves. Cancer gives the children and families a seemingly instantaneous bond even though many of these children and families would not necessarily interact with one another "down the mountain" due to their various differences. As one of our parents put it, "Families at Camp just get it."

In our quantitative survey, parents responding to the question "How many new families in similar situations as yours did you meet at Camp?" the answers ranged from "1" to "over 100"; approximately one-third of respondents, however, stated numbers in the 5-10 range. From this we can deduce that although our respondents represented a diverse array of racial and socio-economic groups, at Camp they find common ground in their journey through cancer. Our quantitative data also indicates that a majority of families stay connected with one or more of the families they meet at Camp. In responding to the question "How many of those families have you connected with since Camp?" approximately 74% of respondents indicated 1 or more; only 26% indicated "none" or "0."

A parent shared that Family Camp was the first time they met a family with a child who had the same diagnosis as her son. For this parent, this connection was significant in that it showed them they were not alone, that this could happen to anyone. As they shared, "Our connection with these families is priceless." Another family, shared that Camp has reshaped their view of the LGBTQ community. Where they were once reluctant to commune with anyone who identifies as LGBTQ, they now embrace everyone they meet at Camp. In fact, they shared that their Camp experience was so transformative that they decided to leave their church because of the exclusionary doctrine (against the LGBTQ community) it preaches. Another parent, described how cancer unites their family to other families despite geographical distances. They shared that they regularly visit other families who live farther than 50 miles away from them to stay connected.

Significance

Given that cancer is a unifier, we see that creating a safe space for community and fellowship along the cancer journey is powerful. For the 26% of families who reported not staying connected to any of the other families they met at Camp, we have identified possible responses such as creating an online forum for parents and hosting quarterly family meetings at the RMHCSC houses as an additional touch point for parents (see below). While some might suggest that programming should be tailored to address the differences between campers, it's not necessary because campers feel relieved to be in a community where others understand their experience with cancer, regardless of other differences in their lives. Camp's role then is to create a culture of inclusivity where families are able to heal and return to a renewed sense of normalcy.

Possible Responses

- ➢ Check in with families who only come to camp once to determine why they've made the decision not to return.
  - Questions to these family would focus on ways to meet their needs better and probe to ensure they felt included and part of the community.
- ➢ Create an online forum for parents.
- ➢ Host quarterly family meetings at the RMHCSC houses as an additional touch point for parents.

Finding 3: What If? What If? What If?

Key Insight: Although navigating through childhood cancer/and survivorship creates stress and isolation, Camp creates a community of support and teaches families how to move beyond "what if, what if, what if."

Description

As one parent explained, childhood cancer puts families on an emotional roller coaster. There are so many unknowns that can send parents into a tailspin of fear. Camp provides parents and children with tools to remain present and focused on the moment. Program elements such as walking in nature, playing games, being disconnected from technology, and spending quite time together outside of the normal daily responsibilities gives campers an opportunity to practice self-care and mindful engagement in present activities as opposed to worried thinking.

Evidence of this finding was expressed when they shared their emotional distress at learning that their son's recent urine test revealed abnormalities. When they began to ask themselves, "what if questions," they found grounding in their son's ability to calmly face their upcoming meeting with his doctor to discuss the test results. Their son expressed his own conviction that no matter what the results, they could handle dealing with them. This parent credits Camp with giving their son this ability to be confident and remain present without spiraling into worries about the future.

Though all of the families we interviewed expressed a significant decrease in stress during and soon after Camp, they did express the need for suggestions and ways to implement Camp activities that reduces stress into their daily family life. Camp is very effective, however, in helping families ease back into a normal daily rhythm even as they continue to face cancer. This is evidenced by the fact that in responding to the question "How true is the following statement? I am more confident in my ability to resume normal life activities as a result of camp," nearly 52% of respondents answered "extremely."

Significance

This finding is significant because Camp program elements instill mindfulness in campers which has a domino effect within families. Children are able to pass their stress reduction techniques to their parents and vice versa. This helps to reduce pain and isolation within families, so that no one family member is carrying their load alone.

Possible Responses

➢ Create a test workshop/presentation at one Summer Camp session and one Family Camp session provided by FSS where they focus on stress relieving/mindfulness techniques that can be used down the mountain.

➢ At Family Camp closing ask parents to share how they plan to take some of the practices they've learned and participated in at Camp when they go home.

➢ Provide families with a one sheet that gives ideas on integrating family unifying activities into their daily lives.

➢ Have families pair up and commit to one goal around mindfulness and one goal around family unity, share those goals with each other, and set a check in date when families will follow up with each other to hold each other accountable to those goals.

Finding 4: Where Healing Happens

Key Insight: Camp is as much a part of the cancer healing process as surgery, chemo therapy, radiation, and various other treatment modalities.

Description

Interviewees referenced suffering from Pediatric Traumatic Medical Stress and that though cancer is in the body of one child, the entire family is impacted by the disease. Not only must children heal from the cancer in their own bodies, but siblings and parents must heal from the trauma of diagnosis, treatment and survivorship as well. One parent shared that "Camp was where my healing process started," since it was where they could first talk about their deepest, most intimate feelings. Our quantitative data suggest that Camp is instrumental in helping others discover a new comfort level in discussing aspects of their cancer journey. When asked the question "How much more comfortable are you with talking to other families about your struggles, challenges, and fears since coming to Camp?" the largest percentage of respondents (just over 42%) responded "a lot." And another parent shared that although their son missed years of schooling due to cancer treatment, his son is mentally and emotionally able to perform at grade level because of the confidence, advocacy skills, and determination he learned at Camp.

Significance

Our data reveal the importance of the mind body connection and the power of Camp to be a critical healing modality for children who would otherwise experience physical, mental and emotional developmental delays. Healing is equally important for siblings and parents who suffer from emotional and psychological trauma because of the cancer diagnosis and treatment since they serve as a child's primary support network. When asked the question "How true is the following statement? Now that I've attended Camp, I am able to manage my daily stress levels," only 4% of respondents said "not at all." This is particularly noteworthy because in responding to the question "How true is the following statement? Before coming to Camp, I was able to manage my daily stress levels." nearly 15% of respondents replied "not at all" – a much larger percentage.

The data show that the pediatric oncology community would benefit from recognizing the strong connection between the mind and the body as children and their families heal from cancer and using the camp modality as part of the patient and families' care plan. Furthermore, toward this end, our volunteer doctors and nurses are at the front lines of taking their learnings from Camp and sharing them with colleagues to transform the practice of pediatric oncology within their field.

Possible Responses

> ➤ Further explore ways to formalize a medical volunteer ambassador program that helps promote the healing value of Camp.

➤ Create an awareness building campaign that shares the healing impact of Camp.
- • Social media focused 30 second videos that provide campers an opportunity to share how Camp has impacted their healing process.
- • Before and After posts on social media.

➤ Present at medical conferences to talk about how and why Camp is a critical part of the healing process.

➤ Identify medical researchers within our volunteer base who might be willing to assist us in publishing Camp's findings around how the Camp experience contributes to a child's healing from cancer.

Finding 5: Inspired Authenticity

Key Insight: The program inspires youth to discover and be their best authentic selves and teach others to be and do the same.

Description

The data reveal that campers are provided with tools and an environment that empowers them to build confidence, safely push past their fears, embrace their true selves and create space where others can do the same. One example given was by one parent who shared that their son had a new found confidence and an ability to advocate for himself in school. His teachers have in turn remarked that it is a pleasure to have him in class. Camper parent shared that they see a huge difference in themselves since coming to Camp. Here children are "leaders amongst their friends" and, as a result, they all have a "brighter future." Their daughter, in particular has tried new sports she would otherwise not have tried and even advocated that she be given additional opportunities before being cut from team. Once she was cut from the team, her parent shared, "The 'failure' did not devastate her because at Camp she learned as long as you tried, that's what counts. Camp did that for her."

One parent shared that Camp has changed how she believes her son should be treated. The inclusivity that defines Camp's programming is now the gold standard for this parent and their family. When their now homeschooled son (do to his increasing physical needs), was not included in his 6th grade class' graduation ceremony, this parent contacted the principal and let them know this is not acceptable. They credit Camp with helping them realize what their son deserves and the importance of advocating on his behalf. Our quantitative data reveal that other parents have also discovered a newfound confidence in their ability to advocate for their children. When asked the question "How true is the following statement? I am a better advocate for my child and family since leaving Camp." the largest percentage of parents (just over 40%) responded with "extremely." And when asked the question "What is one thing you've done to advocate for your child or family since coming to Camp?" survey respondents revealed that their advocacy not only relates to their child's care (i.e. "Speak up more to doctors when I'm concerned about something") but also larger systems change (i.e. "I've been less afraid advocating for the full cleanup of the Santa Susana Field Lab.").

One camper parent shared that their son gains more confidence in himself each year by going to Camp. This parent said, "There's a comfort in knowing someone is always there for him. There is no other place he has in his life where he can be like that. He's starting to branch out and get more independent at Camp. He's gaining confidence that he's actually someone. The counselors care and make him feel that he is somebody – someone to actually care besides mom and dad shows he's actually worth it." Our quantitative data reveal that the confidence that children gain at Camp even inspires their parents to push past their fears about sending them off to week-long summer sessions by themselves once they reach the age of 9 and graduate out of Family Camp. In responding to the question "Have you sent your child to summer camp as a result of having attended Family Camp?" the majority of respondents (nearly 60%) said "yes."

Significance

The intentionality in which programming is implemented—from the vetting and training of volunteers to the inclusion of all campers in activities regardless of physical or mental abilities, to name a few—can be used as a model for other youth and family camps. One parent shared that they attended another camp with their son and found the difference notable. He wasn't included in many activities and had they not been present, he would have had a horrible time.

Possible Responses

- ➤ Explore partnerships with other nonprofit organizations to replicate Camp's model.
- ➤ Create a mentorship program where WOLPers or camper graduates support young campers to continue nurturing their growth and development once their down the mountain.
- ➤ Create a "spread the love down the mountain" tip sheet so campers have tools and examples of things they can do in their community to set an example for inclusivity.

Finding 6: Cancer is the Best Worst Thing

Key Insight: Because cancer led our families to Camp, it effectively opened their eyes to possibilities, areas of personal growth and a newly formed family. They credit cancer then for finding these blessings.

Description

The data reveal that families value the friendships they form with other families who are also experiencing childhood cancer. They also expressed how Camp was the first place where they felt an overwhelming sense of love, inclusion, and support. They have been amazed to witness remarkable changes within themselves and their children that they credit to Camp—many of them now see cancer as a hidden blessing as a result. Several families noted that their biological extended family and friends disconnected from them when their child was sick. Camp became a home away from home and a place where many have formed new families and a support network. One parent stated, "We've been through crap. Some parents have lost kids, but we're all on a journey together. We have such a strong Camp family and to be able to go to reunions and sit in circle and say hi and be together…it's priceless. Those are our people."

The experience of attending Family Camp also awakened many of our respondents to the importance of spending quality time with one another. When asked "How much more time do you spend together as a family each week since you came to Camp?" the largest percentage of respondents (just over 48%) stated 4-6 hours. Family Camp also sparks creativity and discovery within the family unit, as is evidenced by responses to the question "What new activities have you tried since Camp in order to spend quality time with one another?" Answers ranged from recreational activities (i.e. "card games, walks, chess, beach day, lunch out" and "we bought a bow and arrow set!) to forming more positive habits (i.e. "cell phone free time.") In other words, families are not only adopting activities they practice at Camp into their daily lives, but they are also implementing Camp's emphasis on eliminating distractions in order to be more present to friends and loved ones.

Significance

It was surprising to hear parent's think of cancer as a blessing considering it is a disease that could end their child's life and results in a life long journey of checkups, latent affects, and uncertainty. This finding underlines the human need for connection and Camp's ability to foster and grow human connection. In a world that is increasingly disconnected because of our modern lifestyle (i.e. divisive politics, technology, time constraints, geographic boundaries, racial/social economic differences, etc.), Camp's culture of unity is profoundly needed and life changing for our families who have added barriers because of childhood cancer.

Possible Responses
- ➤ Create a family ambassador program to help recruit potential new families.
- ➤ Create an online forum for parents.
- ➤ Add a resource tab to our website.
- ➤ Provide families with a resource binder when they first join Camp.
- ➤ Include a resource corner in family newsletter that is distributed currently.
- ➤ Host quarterly family meetings at the RMHCSC houses as an additional touch point for parents.

Steps Forward

The qualitative findings from our evaluation project where informative and inspiring. Camp is also undergoing a needs assessment process which this project will inform. Once we gather the data from the larger needs assessment, we will then determine programmatic changes, shifts, and/or additions we would like to make over the next five years to deepen our impact and best respond to the evolving needs of our community.

San Diego Children's Choir

Carrie Cottriall, Jan Dziewior, Adrienne Markworth
Ruthie Millgard, Sandra Timmons

Organization and Program Overview

The San Diego Children's Choir is a nonprofit organization that was founded in 1990 to provide children with choral music education and performance opportunities that foster performance excellence and collaboration at the highest artistic level, nurturing individual development and creating a foundation for lifelong success. The Choir is the region's oldest and largest choral training program for children, providing music education to over 1,000 children ages 4-18 who represent over 64 zip codes and 144 schools.

What started as a two-level fee-based choir with 42 children has grown to serving more than 1,000 youth through a core performing ensemble program with five progressive choir levels at multiple rehearsal sites, an outreach program for schools with no choral music education programs, an introductory early childhood program, and enriching opportunities to tour the world. 42% of SDCC participants receive tuition-free instruction.

Our five age-based ensemble choirs (grades 1-12) provide high quality training and performance experiences to over 275 children, and those in grades 3-12 will have the opportunity to tour regionally and nationally.

Through our outreach programs, more than 655 children (grades Pre-K-5) receive in-school choral instruction at eight public elementary schools; six of those are Title 1 and receive free instruction. More than 70 children (ages 4-6) receive music instruction through our beginning music exploratory program.

Students are instructed in proper vocal production, musicianship, sight-reading, and music theory, using a Kodály-based curriculum - an approach to teaching music that is child developmental and centered on singing and quality repertoire. Our model is in line with National Standards for Music Education and the content standards for visual and performing arts adopted by the California State Board of Education.

Choristers in our ensemble choirs perform at more than 25 public and private events throughout the year, and SDCC produces biannual concerts and regularly partners with professional organizations such as San Diego Symphony through collaborative concert programs and events.

The intended impact of the choir experience for the choristers is

1. Choristers become confident and engaged musical artists who demonstrate self-efficacy, a growth mindset and resilience.
2. Choristers embrace empathy and interdependence.
3. Choristers develop skills which reinforce academic success.

Evaluation Methodology

The aim of our evaluation was to see what kind and quality of impact the San Diego Children's Choir is having in the students grades six to 12 who are participating in our performance choir program. To understand this, we explored two broad research questions:

1. What kind and quality of impact are we having on this segment of choristers?
2. What aspects of our program are causing this impact?

Over the course of the project, we (a) developed and refined our ideas of intended impact and indicators, (b) designed and implemented a mixed methods outcome evaluation using both qualitative and quantitative means to collect and analyze data, (c) identified findings, and (d) considered the implications to those findings for program improvement and innovation.

This project began with a focus on the work of identifying and clarifying the intended impact of the performance choir program. Once the ideas of impact had been developed, we used the Heart Triangle™ model to identify qualitative and quantitative indicators of impact focused on the mental, behavioral and emotional changes in choristers that indicate we are achieving our impact. We then used these indicators to design a qualitative interview protocol and a quantitative questionnaire to measure our progress toward achieving our intended impact.

Qualitative Data Collection and Analysis

For the qualitative portion of the evaluation, we designed an in-depth interview protocol to gain data about the structural, qualitative changes resulting from our program. We used a purposeful stratified sampling technique to select a representative sample from the population we serve. Our population size was 70 choristers.

Our sample size was 20 and we drew our sample from the following strata of our population:

➢ 19 Chamber Choristers in Grades 10–12
➢ 35 Girl Choristers in Grades 6–9
➢ 16 Boy Choristers in Grades 6–9

All interviewed choristers have participated in choir for three to 11 years. They are of different ethnicities, socioeconomic levels and ages and from different schools and zip codes. Both boys and girls were interviewed.

Our interview team consisted of two staff members, two board members and a chorister parent. All interviewers participated in the

Project Impact cohort meetings and were trained in qualitative data collection and analysis at the Project Impact meetings.

We then convened one-on-one interviews lasting from between 30 minutes to 45 minutes in length with a sample from the identified strata of the population. Interviewers took notes during the interviews and filled in the notes immediately after the interview to obtain a substantive rendering of the interview.

We analyzed the data inductively using a modified version of thematic analysis. Interviewers implemented the first three phases of thematic analysis (becoming familiar with the data, generating initial codes and identifying themes) for each interview. The interviewers familiarized themselves with the data by reviewing the data from each interview four times, each time thinking through a different aspect of what the data reveal about the research question. The data were then bucketed into four categories to serve as an initial set of codes. Finally, initial themes were generated based on the pervasive insights from the data. This process allowed us to interpret the meaning and significance of the data from each interview.

Next, we brought all of the data analyses and initial themes together and implemented the next two phases of thematic analysis (reviewing themes, defining and naming themes). We reviewed the initial themes as a team to identify the overarching themes that emerged from the full scope of our data analysis to illuminate the collective insights and discoveries. We mapped these themes visually and examined them in various ways to gain greater definition of the features of the themes, causes and catalysts of the themes, new or surprising insights related to the themes, and relationships between the themes that were revealed in the data. We then determined the most significant and meaningful discoveries and brought them forward as findings to be described in the final phase of thematic analysis, this report.

Quantitative Data and Analysis

For the quantitative portion of the evaluation, we designed a questionnaire to collect data on our quantitative indicators of impact. We administered this instrument to 70 choristers and had a response of 39, a 56% response rate. The data was analyzed primarily using measures of central tendency. We identified key insights, patterns, and gaps within the data and incorporated these discoveries into the related findings.

The most significant discoveries from this evaluation are described in the findings that follow.

Limitations

We interviewed only 6–12 grade choristers for the study because we wanted to find out about the choristers' experience, not the parents' perception of the experience. Children of this age have more say in the activities in which they participate, which may skew the responses in that participating children may choose to take part in the choir program, that is they are self-selecting in.

Findings

Finding 1: More than Just a Song (Self-efficacy and confidence)
Key Insight: The act of publicly performing the music they have practiced expands a chorister's belief of what they are capable of doing.

Description

Each year choristers in the San Diego Children's Choir spend 30 weeks in rehearsal and perform publicly at least six times. Because of this work it isn't surprising that choristers express comfort in presenting or performing in front of crowds. But this comfort was developed by participating in choir and not from earlier experiences. According to a 6th grade chorister who has been in choir for five years, the experiences in choir "definitely gives me more confidence and I don't get stage fright anymore because I've sung in front of a crowd of like 40,000 people."

Our quantitative data also supported what we heard in our interviews. 75% of choristers said that they are usually or always confident in presenting or performing in front of people as a result of their participation in choir, up from just 34% reporting they usually or always felt confident prior to joining choir.

Figure 1. I am confident in presenting or performing in front of people. (n=38)

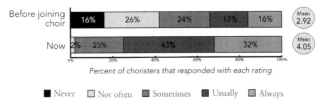

Percent of choristers that responded with each rating

■ Never ☐ Not often ■ Sometimes ■ Usually ■ Always

While experiences of success certainly make up a large portion of self-efficacy development, there is also room for failure, a point noted by many of the choristers interviewed. Participants shared stories that reflected on how they handle making mistakes; unilaterally all choristers that responded reframed these mistakes as a learning experience.

As one chorister stated, "Just being able to know, no matter how much you practice or you work on this, something may still go wrong and you need to think on your feet and you need to figure it out."

In interviews, we heard how choristers had a sense of self-accountability in meeting the demands of training for each performance when faced with learning repertoire and other training challenges. One chorister shared, "Something that's difficult about choir is that you want to point out mistakes but you really just need to take responsibility for yourself and sing through the frustration."

Our quantitative data revealed that 87% of choristers stated they feel obligated or very obligated to be prepared for rehearsal. (n=39)

Stories demonstrate support for others as musicians as they learned together, which lessened individual fears of failure and built confidence. They also demonstrated individual responsibility when rising to new challenges.

One chorister shared that she did not let failures get in the way of success saying, "[I have] confidence that even if I mess up, that not to come after myself…but understand that everyone around me won't be upset. Everyone messes up, and everyone around me is supportive."

A common thread throughout our interviews was that individual choristers need to adjust thoughtfully and strategically to changing situations and challenges during training and performances to be successful.

One chorister shared, "We definitely need to work on artistic expression; I sometimes forget dynamics and phrasing and blending with other people and making a unified sound and not just volume." and another said, "I think being aware of everyone else around you because it's so easy to get lost in your own sound so it's easy to make it a mess if you don't pay attention."

Many choristers also shared that the growth in their confidence translated outside of choir to school and other activities. One chorister reflected on their experience in Choir, "Choir gives you a taste of how good it can be when you achieve something and it kind of makes you want to be just as good in other areas of your life." Another shared a similar thought, "It gives me more confidence when I'm trying new things."

Our quantitative data showed that most choristers are developing this confidence to try new things. 69% of choristers reported they usually or always felt comfortable trying something new even if they might not do it well the first time. This represented a 116% increase from how frequently they reported feeling comfortable trying new things before they joined Choir.

Figure 2. I feel comfortable trying something new even if I might not do it well the first time. (n=39)

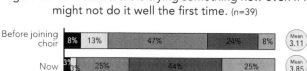

Before joining choir   8%   13%   47%   24%   8%   Mean 3.11

Now   3%   25%   44%   25%   Mean 3.85

Percent of choristers that responded with each rating

■ Never   □ Not often   ▨ Sometimes   ■ Usually   ▨ Always

61

Significance

Children and youth with a strong sense of self-efficacy are more likely to challenge themselves with difficult tasks and be intrinsically motivated. These students will put forth a high degree of effort in order to meet their commitments, and attribute failure to things which are in their control, rather than blaming external factors. Self-accountability and resilience are results. These traits are highly correlated with academic success and consistent employment, so time spent in choir can increase choristers' likelihood of success in school and life.

Flinding 2: Do you hear what I hear? (Listening)

Key Insight: To create a great sound choristers must listen louder than they sing - listen to each other, to their director and to the music.

Description

By definition a choir is a group of voices; a good choir is a group of voices melded together to create one sound, a point choristers shared multiple times. As one chorister put it,

> [What's hardest is] unifying. Making sure everyone has the same sound and making sure the harmonies are correct because everyone in this choir has an AMAZING voice by themselves but sometimes just getting it together is the hardest part. Listening. Taking a step back and singing quieter sometimes so I can listen to people around me and try to match what they're doing.

The data reflects a consistency amongst those interviewed of the importance they place on this skill. A ten-year chorister reported,

> You need to listen to your part in relationship to other harmonies in the mix...are you pitching accurately, are you in synch time-wise with the other part, does it sound 'off' at all, are you drowning them out or are you in perfect balance? There is so much you have to think about.

Our quantitative data (n= 39) supports the observations of the choristers; 77% said they often or always employ "listening louder than they sing" and 87% said the were aware or very aware of listening to each other to adjust their sound as needed.

Another chorister shared a real-time example,

> I think it was the winter concert last year where we were singing and the alto section got completely off or we did something wrong where half of us got lost from the actual group. Lost in the music. We must have missed a rhythm or verse because all of a sudden, we were in a different place than the rest of the choir. It was just a thing about listening. We all got just kind of quiet, which is weird, we just listened to where they were and joined back in slowly and I think that was a test of us being able to listen to the OTHER groups rather than push on singing our part wrong which would have been a bigger disaster. We just listened and then joined in.

Significance

Listening is key to all effective communication. Without the ability to listen effectively it is easy to misunderstand what others are saying and communication breaks down.

As one chorister shared,

> [The director] says listen louder than you sing. Not just when you sing but be optimistic and listen to other people's opinions and views and working together." Another chorister shares, "… now I'm learning to sing as a group, I'm developing into a musician and I'm learning to listen to others' voices, learning to grow and change. It changes how I think about myself because I've always been a person who has trouble in groups at school. I'm stubborn and I don't like to compromise my ideas. But in choir, the music is there and there's nothing [else.]

The United States Department of Labor Secretary's Commission on Achieving Necessary Skills (SCANS) identified five competencies and three foundation skills that are essential for those entering the workforce. Listening skills were among the foundation skills SCANS identified as being critical.

Most choristers will not become professional musicians, but the skills, like listening, they learn while in choir will carry with them throughout their lives.

Finding 3: "Choir is a team sport that's not a sport" (Teamwork)
Key Insight: Choristers view choir as a collaborative, cooperative group of singers who must work like a team to create the results they want.

Description

Choral singing is by its very nature a cooperative venture. Each individual must be aware of and stay in sync with the choristers around them. The importance of this cooperation and teamwork was mentioned by many of our choristers. A chorister who has been in choir for nine years explains, "There is a lot of cooperative teamwork because you can't have one voice stick out amongst all of them. You have to all unify into one and I think that's really important." Another shared, "Through choir I've learned to cooperate with people who are my friends and people who are not my friends. It's like a team sport, but it's not a sport."

For some, choir provided a concrete goal (perfecting a piece of music) that provided an opportunity to let go of their egos and experience true teamwork and cooperation. One boy in middle school expressed it like this: "It helps that you HAVE to work together to get a goal done. You know you want this goal but sometimes you have different ways of doing it so you need to compromise."

Another middle school boy shared that choir helped him learn that his idea didn't always have to be the best for him to enjoy working with others.

For others, success in choir meant they were more likely to take responsibility for their work. Another chorister said, "Before, if the group wasn't doing anything I wouldn't take the initiative. Now, I take the initiative." Choristers frequently described success as a group during a performance or rehearsal.

During interviews, we did not hear comments like "I was successful because I was chosen for the solo." Instead, we heard comments like, "We were successful because we finally sang a difficult piece well," or "We recovered from a mistake at the Holiday Pops."

While choristers spent a large part of their interviews talking about their own experiences, their own strengths and weaknesses, they framed their success in terms of the group. They articulated the crucial balance of being personally prepared and skilled, but using "we" and "us" when talking about success. Their true joy came from the group perfecting a piece, even though they felt satisfaction at their contribution. As one chorister shared, "You are there, and you've been doing [choir] for so long. You know it and the people around you know it. It is a group mentality. We can do this together. We're not alone."

Significance

For students who are not drawn to traditional athletic sports, this is an important finding to show that the experience of youth teamwork is not confined to the athletic fields. Teamwork is an activity in which members of an organization come together to work toward a common goal or set of goals and singing in a choir fits this definition well. As choristers mature they will use this skill in school and at work. Regardless of the job, employers want to hire people who are team players who are cooperative and work well with others.

Finding 4: Tears of sadness, songs of joy (Emotional well-being)
Key Insight: Singing in the choir makes choristers more attuned to their emotions, both positive and negative.

Description

An abundance of research has shown that singing in a choir increases feelings of well-being–an observation made by many choristers during our interviews. But perhaps more importantly, we heard from choristers who described their experience of becoming more comfortable with their negative emotions as well. Choristers said that singing sad songs, such as the spiritual Deep River, gave them an opportunity to connect not only with a different part of our country's history but the deep sadness of a human story. One student described her experience, "I knew about slavery, but when we really looked at the lyrics and realized what these people experience, it was overwhelming. I can't imagine preferring death …." Another said, "…. I would cry while singing this song."

Our quantitative data confirmed what choristers shared about their well-being in their interviews. 79% of choristers reported that they usually or always have a feeling of overall well-being now as compared with only 55% of students reporting that they usually or always had this feeling before joining choir.

Figure 3. I have a feeling of overall well-being.

Before joining choir: 13% | 32% | 45% | 10% — Mean 3.52

Now: 3% | 18% | 51% | 28% — Mean 4.04

Percent of choristers that responded with each rating

■ Never   □ Not often   ■ Sometimes   ■ Usually   ▨ Always

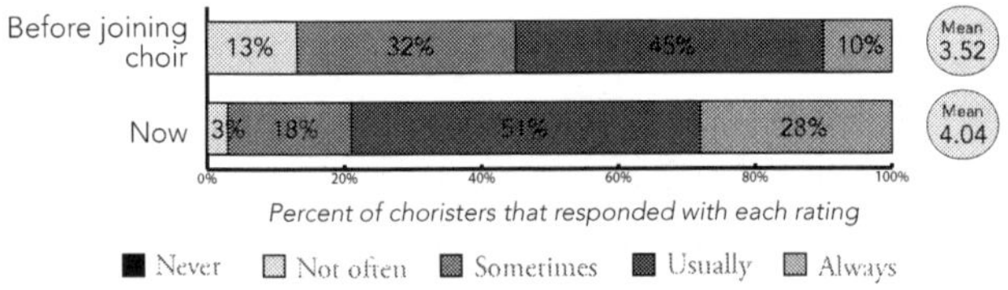

Our quantitative survey also revealed that all choristers reported feeling joy from singing and 74% of them reported that they always feel joy from singing.

In our interviews we also heard that being together in this process and sharing the experiences make it doable and worthwhile. As one chorister shared, "You are there, and you've been doing [choir] for so long. You know it and the people around you know it. It is a group mentality. We can do this together. We're not alone." Another chorister said, "I've learned that within the music of other cultures there's a deeper meaning to it." And a third shared that the music made her feel more connected, she says, "It's crazy to think that this is something someone wrote 100 or 200 years ago. It's still being sung today. Kind of crazy to think about it."

Significance

For many preteens and teens, it is a time of emotional extremes; feelings come in waves and are hard to process. Singing in a group helps them with emotional regulation and normalization of negative feelings. Choristers realize that they are not the only ones who have these feelings, and that sharing the experience with others makes it all seem more real but less daunting–their feelings are affirmed but don't overwhelm them. As a chorister of three years observed, "Everything is not about you, other people have different points of view and I can learn to understand those points of view and how they feel about things."

Finding 5: San Diego's Ambassadors of Song (Unique Opportunities)

Key Insight: Having the opportunity to perform in professional venues with professional musicians and to travel with the choir increases choristers' understanding of their place in the larger world and their ability to successfully maneuver in it.

Description

Our interviews highlighted how unique performance and tour opportunities developed choristers as musicians and individuals. Choristers shared stories about the positive impact of performances at Carnegie Hall and with the San Diego Symphony. As one chorister said,

> The choir makes me feel like I am more of a part of San Diego, it ties us into the city and explore more of the musical side. For example, being able to sing with Westwind Brass and the San Diego Symphony. Singing with Maestro Patel, it forms a bond and we start to feel like we are a part of the musical community

of San Diego. I just joined the choir to sing, but this is an added
bonus.

The high expectations of such experiences advanced their musical
development. As one chorister stated, "The experience of singing with
SDCC gives me unique and powerful opportunities that I wouldn't
otherwise have. I feel I'm more a part of San Diego because we sing in
so many different places."

Choristers also reflected on experiences as new musicians and
genres of music and the respect they developed for other cultures.
One chorister expressed herself this way,

> This semester we're doing a bunch of music from different cul-
> tures. We're doing an African American spiritual, a piece from
> the Philippines …That's what I love about it. We have a jazz
> piece, and also singing excerpts from an opera. I mean the mu-
> sic here is insanely diverse. We do get to learn about the story
> behind the song and also the language since to learn it you need
> to be able to sing in that language. You get to learn the pronun-
> ciations and you kind of can almost speak a few sentences in
> another language…

In reflecting on how she thinks about other cultures a high school
chorister said, "They are all unique but [it shows] we all have the
same kind of underlying principles and ideas."

"I feel like I'm part of something bigger. With the choir I can
perform and do things that make me happy. I feel like I'm doing
something important."

Significance

These interviews gave us further insights into the depth these formative
experiences provide. These unique opportunities gave many of these
choristers a sense of belonging, a sense of pride in being a member
of an accomplished choir. The performance experiences connected

them with the San Diego arts and cultural community through the interaction they experience with new audiences. It challenged them to do better and gave them a sense of pride. Having found a place to fit in and give back, choristers understand that they have many places and ways to create a life for themselves. Their world is larger than their family, their school or even San Diego. And it is a world they are willing to embrace.

Finding 6: Practice makes perfect and perfect practice makes a great performance (Hard Work = Success)

Key Insight: To create a good choral sound all singers need to know the repertoire, blend their voices and be highly synchronized. As choristers prepare and consistently practice for a performance; they work to sing without errors. Over time they come to realize that hard work pays off.

Description

Children may be born with a positive response to musical sounds, but like learning a language, reading music notation and creating a musical sound takes time and effort. Choristers expressed an understanding that focused and consistent work is necessary to learn and perform their music. When they describe the process of getting a new piece of music and struggling with sight reading it, then memorizing it, they fully comprehend the effort that is necessary for the outcome they desire.

A chorister explains why he loves the performances, "Because there's that achievement because we've worked on them for so long and finally there's something that ends up happening."

As one chorister explained,

> We have things we have to memorize each week and that's honestly a big push. You need motivation because you can tell when people put in the work – how hard work like when you get a piece of music that at the beginning of the semester you

can barely get through and turn into this beautiful thing and that's a big motivation.

Significance

Choral singing skills are developed over time, with many stumbles and errors, but choristers who are successful develop a persistence that transfers to other areas of a chorister's life. As one chorister put it, "It makes me very passionate about succeeding in other areas of life because success is hard, is hard work, but the things are going to make you happy, you need to put work in to get something out."

Another said, "I'm so much more motivated to work on things now knowing that the outcomes can be great. The work may seem hard but the outcomes can be super amazing and beneficial."

Finding 7: Move from Making Music to Making Music I Like ("Hey, I actually sound pretty good!")

Key Insight: Choristers at this level participate because they love to sing, but choir participation gave them the opportunity to sing well.

Description

Our interviews highlighted how singing well became important to our choristers. While choristers at this level all participate because they love to sing, they did not begin with the confidence that they were producing a beautiful sound. One chorister shared, "I always liked to sing, but I didn't like the way my voice sounded." Students shared that through the SDCC experience they increasingly liked the sound they were able to produce.

Our quantitative data (n=39) supports this observation. 85% of choristers responding said that they often or always think about appropriate use of breath energy when singing while 80% said they often or always think about use of yawn/resonant space while singing.

This change did not happen overnight. One chorister described it as a five-year journey: "I started in fourth grade but it wasn't until 9th grade that I was like 'Wooo, my voice changed!' Even my mom said my voice had really improved."

Other choristers, especially the older high school students, described their skills more specifically, recognizing their emerging ability to add dynamics, phrasing, and musicality. Choristers readily identified when their ability matched their enjoyment. An eleven-year chorister explained it as finding your voice, being able to express yourself by using all the skills you have learned and communicating to your audience.

As a six-year chorister stated, "I feel like I am part of something bigger. With the choir I can perform and do things that make me happy. I feel like I'm doing something important."

Additionally, choristers were straightforward and humble about their challenges and gifts. Although these students are immersed in a media culture that often highlights quick fixes, technological shortcuts, and over-the-top prodigies featured on reality shows, they demonstrated the power of combining passion with patient work. As one chorister put it, "Small accomplishments are rehearsing a harmony in practice. It's hard sometimes and takes time. But then you get it."

Significance

It is not surprising that being trained to sing in a choir produces quality singers, nor is it surprising that those who participate in choir enjoy singing. What is significant is that the choristers were able to give such specifics about their experience of learning and improvement, and they were able to articulate the experience of growing into their passion.

As one chorister said, "I'm proud of the performances. They are really unique experiences that set us apart from the crowd. Carnegie Hall is somewhere where soloists work their whole lives to sing at but we were able to do it as a group." Added another, "The experience of singing for SDCC gives me unique and powerful opportunities that I wouldn't otherwise have."

Conclusion

Insights into Impact

Based on research of music and the child, and experiences of other youth choral organizations, we expected to see our choristers becoming confident and engaged musical artists who developed a sense of self-efficacy, a growth mindset and resilience. Our evaluation supported this to a great degree. Choristers are aware of the amount of hard work necessary to perform a polished program and know that it doesn't happen overnight. They realize how much they need to collaborate with other choristers and be real team members when they practice and perform. They learn to apply the vocal skills, real time, and to be aware of and listen to other singers around them. Most choristers interviewed did not refer to themselves as musical artists but acknowledged that they are developing a sound that they like and of which they are proud both as individuals and as a group.

Because choir repertoire reflects different genres, cultures, countries and time periods we predicted that choristers would develop greater appreciation for the diversity of each other and San Diego which would promote empathy and understanding of our interdependence. Most choristers interviewed did not express this idea.   Most didn't talk about increased cultural sensitivity or appreciation of different cultures but talked about the team work developed in the choir community and how much that community means to them - they are oblivious to where other choristers come from (accepting and collaborative). They see themselves as part of something bigger and focus how much they mean to one another and how they feel free to make mistakes without being shamed or shaming others. They talk of real connection with each other and their directors. The focus was on commonality and not on their differences.

Finally, we hypothesized that choristers develop skills that reinforce academic success. No chorister interviewed spoke about school work but talked about wanting to succeed in all they do. The hard work they put in at choir pays off and they know that it will elsewhere if they apply themselves the same way. They also got better at collaborative work at school because of the team work in choir.

Participation in the San Diego Children's Choir gives choristers a sense of accomplishment and belonging. They see themselves as teammates and know that together they can create magnificent music.

Steps Forward

To truly analyze what we mean, we need to put into place a data collecting process to track academic success and changes that might occur during a chorister's tenure in the choir, better measurement of each chorister's music theory competency, and a rubric to track social well being.

We also need to find out what happens to choristers after they graduate from high school (and the choir). Do they go to college and at what rate? How quickly do they graduate, what careers do they choose?

We believe that participation in music and the arts makes it more likely you will be a patron of the arts when you are older. We need to track past choristers to see if they are current patrons of the arts and still part of the arts community.

Future Evaluation Opportunities

Our evaluation focused on one segment of the choir program; the performance choirs. But some of the greatest impacts of choral singing happens at earlier ages. We will be looking at other programs and assessing the greatest impacts at each stage of choral development.

Early Years programs (4 - 6 years old)

Intro Choirs (1st - 4nd grades)

Training choirs (4th - 6th grades)

Outreach programs (various grades at Title 1 schools)

And in conjunction with neuroscientists at UCSD we are planning a study to look at the impact on pre-literacy/literacy beginning at the PreK level. This study will be longitudinal in nature and carry through to the first grade to see if underserved students will be ready to read at grade level.

EDUCATION | CHARACTER DEVELOPMENT | LEADERSHIP

Pro Kids | The First Tee of San Diego

Alumni Program

Alison Aragon, Michael Oliveri, Said Shaba

Introduction

The mission of Pro Kids | The First Tee of San Diego is to challenge underserved youth to excel in life by promoting character development, life skills, and values through education and the game of golf. Through a unique set of programs that combine sport, study, and service, we provide youth, grades 2 - 12, with equitable access to opportunities that will set them on the path to success in adulthood. With college and career programming and direct support scholarships for program alumni, the vision of our founder Ernest H. Wright continues to ring true: "golf is the hook; education is the payoff." Since 1994, we have seen over 20,000 kids transform through the values intrinsic to the game of golf—honesty, confidence, and respect—and since 1999, we have awarded almost $2.2 million to 250 scholars, most of whom are the first in their families to pursue higher education.

The program we chose to evaluate does not yet exist. While we began this process with the intention of reconnecting with our alumni, this impact investigation helped us to see the need for a formalized alumni group that can support one another, and that we as an organization can continue to support as they continue on the path to success. The Pro Kids Scholarship program acts as a bridge between the organization and students who have gone through the Pro Kids program. This process helped us understand the lasting impact of being part of the Pro Kids family, and what this identity means to our program alumni. Our findings showed that the life skills learned through the game of golf and at Pro Kids have helped our alumni grow, achieve, and excel in higher education and their careers. It was great to hear about the sense of pride and the willingness to stay involved and mentor the next generation of Pro Kids, but it is now our responsibility to make these experiences open and available to alumni.

Evaluation Methodology

Beginning in January 2018, we undertook an 8-month impact investigation through Project Impact with Dialogues in Action, LLC. The aim of our evaluation was to see what kind and quality of impact we are having on alumni participants of our program. Over the course of the project, we (a) developed and refined our ideas of intended impact and indicators, (b) designed and implemented both qualitative and quantitative means to collect and analyze data, and (c) identified findings and considered the implications of these findings for our program.

Qualitative Data and Analysis

This project began by identifying and clarifying the intended impacts of our program for alumni. Once our intended impacts had been developed, we built questions that would help us measure our impact. For the qualitative portion of the evaluation, we designed an in-depth interview protocol to gain insights about the deeper, qualitative changes that alumni experience as a result of our program.

We then convened one-on-one interviews lasting from between

45 minutes and one hour in length, interviewing 15 alumni in total. Interviewers took notes during the interviews and filled in the notes immediately after the interview to obtain a substantive rendering of the interview.

We analyzed the data inductively using a modified version of thematic analysis. Interviewers implemented the first three phases of thematic analysis (becoming familiar with the data, generating initial codes and identifying themes) for each interview. The interviewers familiarized themselves with the data by reviewing the data from each interview four times, each time thinking through a different aspect of what the data reveal about the research question. The data were then bucketed into four categories to serve as an initial set of codes. Finally, initial themes were generated based on the pervasive insights from the data. This process allowed us to interpret the meaning and significance of the data from each interview.

Next, we brought all of the data analyses and initial themes together and implemented the next two phases of thematic analysis (reviewing themes, defining and naming themes). We reviewed the initial themes as a team to identify the overarching themes that emerged from the full scope of our data analysis to illuminate the collective insights and discoveries. We mapped these themes visually and examined them in various ways to gain greater definition of the features of the themes, causes and catalysts of the themes, new or surprising insights related to the themes, and relationships between the themes that were revealed in the data. We then determined the most significant and meaningful discoveries and brought them forward as findings to be described in the final phase of thematic analysis, this report.

Quantitative Data and Analysis

For the quantitative portion of the evaluation, we designed a 20-question survey to collect data on our quantitative indicators of impact. We administered this instrument to approximately 25 alumni and had a response rate of 76%, with a total of 19 responses.

Findings

Finding #1: Pro Kids Cares - Pro Kids is a Support System of People You Can Rely On

Description

Throughout our interviews, alumni consistently referenced adults and peers from Pro Kids who served as mentors or helped them in a significant way. Many discussed former staff as the key people in their development at Pro Kids and throughout their college and career experiences. A recent graduate of the master's in education program at the University of San Diego recounts, "One of the staff pushed me to do a speech in 2010 in front of Congress on behalf of the First Tee. I was so scared, but it was great for social/emotional learning." Pro Kids acts as an extended family and brings about a sense of community to its members. Pro Kids is a place to find people you can count on. Tiffany, who also has an older and younger sister in the program believes, "The most important thing is that kids feel supported. Pro Kids doesn't give up on you like other places—it gives you more opportunities, invites you to events, hires you—it is not just a place where you come to learn golf."

We noticed that we got the most emotional and in-depth responses when alumni talked about memories they had out on the course with their friends and coaches. Alumni found that these experiences connected to their current career goals. Pro Kids alumni, staff member, and future lawyer One reflected, "Pro Kids has changed my life. I was very fortunate to grow up as a Pro Kids member, and I owe a lot of my accomplishments to the commitment of the staff members and donors for supporting my vision." The program has historically had a high retention rate, and we have evolved to support our members' journey through education – elementary to middle to high school to college prep to scholarship support. If we can continue to be a support system for kids and their families our future will remain impactful throughout San Diego County and beyond.

Significance

Our late founder Ernie Wright said, "Golf is the hook, education is the payoff." He saw a neighborhood that needed a safe space for kids to go after school and knew that golf would provide the path to learning life lessons and staying on the track to success. His vision was to make a challenging and rewarding sport accessible to youth who normally would not be exposed to it. Much like a family, he saw this place as a third space where kids could gather to learn from one another and built their community around golf. But it has always been about much more than playing the game. It's about teaching life skills, like honesty, respect, and confidence—promoting education and creating a welcoming environment. Pro Kids is a place for all and a support system for our members and their families. Staying true to Ernie's vision as well as evolving to meet the educational needs of our members will ensure that families can rely on Pro Kids for many years to come.

Responses

We want to keep Pro Kids a place where kids feel safe, supported, and pushed to their potential. But creating loyalty to the organization as a whole instead of staff members will be a challenge moving forward. To acknowledge and address this challenge, we are considering emphasizing community collaboration, partnerships, and resource sharing to enhance Pro Kids' all-around services in the lives of current members and as they transition into alumni. To achieve this, we will:

- ➢ Invite other service organizations the opportunity to set up information booths at our family events
- ➢ Take the opportunity to set up information booths at community and school events
- ➢ Connect families with appropriate services and resources
- ➢ Invite organizations to utilize our facility

Finding #2: #PKAllDay – Pro Kids Pride Runs Deep

Description

Alumni described a great sense of pride in being a Pro Kid. Many discussed Pro Kids as a unique place with a unique mission that helped shape them as individuals. As they were being introduced to the game, they were also being introduced to lifelong friends. This is something they truly cherish. Not only did alumni speak of their accomplishments during our interviews, but they also discussed their friend's successes on and off the course as members and after high school. One Pro Shop Starter and program alumni say, "Honestly, wow, Pro Kids is like my second family. I grew up here. When I see other alumni coming through or out in the world, it is like seeing my brothers and sisters. I love this place."

This finding was also confirmed in our survey. When asked if they feel connected to their community as a result of their participation in ProKids, 16 out of 19 alumni agreed or strongly agreed.

Figure 1. I feel connected to community.

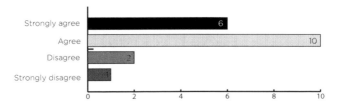

Significance

Pro Kids has value beyond its programming. Lifelong friends are made because of Pro Kids. "I hated golf when I first started, but I ended up making a lot of friends and wanted to come back. Furthermore, the network our members build at Pro Kids impacts their college experience and careers in many cases.

Responses

How do we utilize this pride to honor our past, enhance our present, and support our future? A focus on alumni-driven events or workshops will connect the generations of Pro Kids and build out the Pro Kids network more as we move into our 25th year of programming. Additionally, our messaging can focus on specific impact stories of our alumni. Communicating different paths of success in the community - in business, in education, on the golf course, and beyond -will help translate this pride into a greater connection between the different generations of Pro Kids.

Figure 2. I am a better leader.

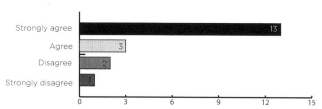

Finding #3: It's Bigger Than Golf– Pro Kids is an Environment that Truly Teaches Life Skills

Description

At Pro Kids, we have 18 "Words to Live By," or character values that we instill in our participants. Alumni mentioned several of these values throughout the interviews. Although some alumni do not play golf anymore, the life skills that they learned at Pro Kids have guided them throughout their education and careers.

Any skilled golfer must possess confidence, commitment, and discipline. This confidence grows from an eagerness to learn and a commitment to practice and put in the work. Many of our alumni connected their growth in confidence at Pro Kids to their academic experience. They discussed how the impact of their journey on the course helped them in the classroom. One alumnus talked about his persistence and tireless work with his driver. "At Pro Kids and Colina Park, you spend a lot of time working on your short game. My driver was really holding me back when I started to play bigger courses, and I struggled for a while. I can say with confidence that my driver became my best club because I was committed to making the weakest part of my game my strongest."

Pro Kids alumni referenced their improvement with public speaking and comfort level meeting new people networking and during events. They both talked about the value of strong communication skills as they continue their studies and gain experience through internships. They see it as a real strength when they begin their careers.

In our survey, every participant agreed that Pro Kids helped them communicate with confidence.

Figure 3. I communicate with confidence.

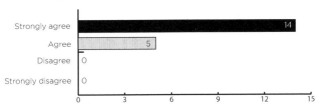

Pro Kids alumni consistently discussed the program as a place where they respected their coaches, the staff, and especially their peers. They felt a responsibility to play the game the right way and welcome new members. Simple, respectful gestures and traits, such as introducing yourself proudly, giving a firm handshake, and making eye contact go a long way in making great first impressions.

Golf is inherently a difficult game that requires mental and physical discipline and perseverance, but the social interaction with adults at a young age, communication skills, group collaboration, learned at Pro Kids proved to be just as valuable as any golf skills. Pro Kids provides an environment for kids to stay true to themselves and display the honesty and integrity that will help them excel on the course and in life. In the game of golf, you have to take responsibility for your choices, your frame of mind, and the way you conduct yourself on the course. It is a game that mirrors life, which teaches you to "enjoy the journey, enjoy the people you meet, and be yourself."

Significance

Our members benefit most from the education and life skills they receive through training in golf. While we would love to produce a ton of professional golfers, the foundation of our success has a large alumni base who have become dedicated and successful professionals and community leaders. One reflected, "I see golf as less of a sport and more of a way to get to know someone better and build new relationships."

Responses

Life skills significantly contribute to success. Pro Kids can continue to evolve and promote more social interaction with adults, collaboration with other organizations, and exposure to different creative and educational experiences at a younger age. Our boys' and girls' mentoring initiatives connect board members and donors with our young members. Additionally, Pro Kids has hosted a young writer's workshop for members and the youth in the surrounding community. To maximize these experiences for our kids, we look forward to:

Coordinating more career workshops and visits to San Diego-based company headquarters to expose our mentees to potential career paths.

➤ Increasing the number of home and home tournaments where Pro Kids and country club members play at each other's home courses. This will allow more Pro Kids the opportunity to have these adult interactions and create connections.

➤ Inviting elementary school age members to come to events and be more involved as ambassadors for the program

➤ Incorporating more member presentations to the board, at community events, and their peers

Finding #4: Paying it Forward – Pro Kids Alumni Express Interest in Becoming Mentors

Description

Pro Kids alumni want to give back. Their appreciation for their mentors inspires them to become mentors for the new generation of Pro Kids or impact whichever community they live in. This is not surprising as we heard several stories of different Pro Kids staff, donors, and board members playing significant roles in the development of alumni interviewees. One of our Pro Kids alumni was introduced to the program by one of our board members. As she made new friends and progressed through the program, the board member became her mentor, invited her to experiences at country clubs and community events, and encouraged her to become involved in Toastmasters. She referenced this special relationship in her interview and said, "I am so grateful for her and her guidance. My focus now is on my coursework at UC Santa Barbara, and I have a lot to accomplish when I start my career, but I want to be in that next generation of Pro Kids mentors."

Significance

This is a large part of the legacy of the organization and the fact that alumni expressed interest in paying it forward is so meaningful. Board members, donors, and volunteers have been instrumental in as mentors and beyond. In the early days of the organization, we had no formal scholarship structure or program. Many donors and board members had meaningful connections with Pro Kids individuals and financially supported their college experience. As the scholarship program became more formalized and interactions between supporters and kids became more frequent, our members found mentors from all different backgrounds. We consider our next phase is to add more recent alumni to our mentor network to create a combination of established professionals and young professionals.

Responses

Pro Kids can help foster these mentorship opportunities for our alumni and current members. The organization will play a crucial role in fostering a diverse network of mentors available to meet the needs of our members and provide opportunity. We want to create small events to match young mentors with alumni mentees. This will enable us to meet the needs of our alumni while providing mentorship to our current Pro Kids members. By creating a platform for mentorship, we can keep the alumni engagement high as well as meet the growing needs of our current members.

Mentorship and lasting bonds can be formed by organizing tee times, fun field trips, and service projects. We also can experiment by combining our existing mentoring initiatives with our established donor base to our new alumni mentor network. This could potentially connect alumni with previous mentors or contacts that they haven't seen in years as well. By providing Alumni support, we can instill a tradition of mentorship by meeting the needs of different generations. Alumni can be connected to the donors and in the process pass on their lessons to our younger members. This will ensure that our programs key message is being conveyed to everyone.

Finding #5: Return of the Alumni – Build a Bridge for Former Members to Re-engage with the Organization.

Description

The skills, friendships, and memories alumni have experienced because of Pro Kids are truly important to them. From our interviews, we learned that strengthening our communication and engagement with alumni after they are out of the program is an area for our organization to grow. One of the primary takeaways from this evaluation is that we need to re-engage our former members in a meaningful way.

Interviewees expressed the desire to stay involved but a sense of feeling disconnected with current programs and newer staff. Our alumni desire more follow-up from Pro Kids, events to keep them connected, and more opportunity to do the things they loved to do as members. For example, one alumnus described "I had a lot of fun when I met with people from other chapters at an event when I was an active Pro Kid. The Chapters are all so different; it would be great to have the opportunity to network with other alumni throughout the US." Another commented, "I would like to volunteer during college breaks, but there are never any opportunities specific to that time period (when I am back in San Diego)."

Significance

Alumni success and engagement is an indicator of our success. Our 25th anniversary is next year, which presents a great opportunity to re-engage and celebrate our alumni, who can serve as mentors to our current members/scholars and even become future donors and board members. The organization will benefit in the long-term by creating an effective alumni engagement strategy and executing it appropriately.

Responses

We are considering the following possible initiatives that will help us achieve better communication and engagement with alumni:

- ➤ Create a Pro Kids Alumni Facebook group
- ➤ Stay connected to our Alumni base through social media is an easy way to communicate with a large number of people. This can happen by posting regularly to group pages
- ➤ Host an annual alumni event/reunion at Pro Kids
- ➤ Hosting annual events can be a great place for Alumni to network and stay in communication with not just Pro Kids, but with each other.
- ➤ Invite Alumni to Home & Home Tournaments (current Pro Kids members, country club members, and alumni play on full-size golf courses together).

This will provide a platform to keep Alumni connected to the mission through the activity that had a lasting impact on their lives (GOLF).

Conclusion

Our intended goal of this research was to understand how we could continue to keep our program alumni engaged with the community. From the data that was collected, it is evident that our alumni want more opportunities to be engaged. This is, in part, because of our program curriculum. Our curriculum encourages members to be invested in their community from a young age. This is something that we have to facilitate for our alumni by inviting them to take part in organized projects and events that are beneficial to City Heights, to Oceanside and Pro Kids. We are close to achieving our goal, but our next step needs to be focused on creating more opportunities for the alumni to contribute their input and time — a goal moving forward to engage students on their way out of the program and re-engage alumni more purposefully to ensure that the Pro Kids network remains strong and impactful.

Steps Forward

The events and fundraising campaigns throughout our 25th year will be focused on the history of the organization, the people who have made it successful, and the future impact we intend to have. This will help our alumni engagement efforts and gain insight into best practices and appropriate strategies moving forward. We are connecting with alumni to hear their impact stories, we are hosting a "Homecoming" on site in January focused on scholars and alumni, and our annual gala in the spring will include original members, past board presidents, past honorees, alumni, etc. Moving forward we hope to capture more updated alumni contact information, facilitate annual networking/events for alumni, and enhance the experience of the current Pro Kids membership by utilizing the talents and experiences of our alumni.

Future Evaluation Opportunities

Evaluations that measure how our events and programs meet our alumni network needs and expectations will be critical during and after of 25th year. An honest assessment of how successful are we are in building that bridge for former members to re-engage with Pro Kids will be necessary for measuring touch points. Amount of information received, events attended, and social media engagement could be a few more ways to evaluate success. Other areas to explore include: Are we providing enough mentoring opportunities? Do alumni feel informed and up to date on the current Pro Kids program and news? Do alumni feel like their input is considered?

Venice Family Clinic

Robert Levine Family Health Center's Teen Clinic

Anasa Matthews, MSW, MPH, Ariel Peterson, MPH
Jonathan Vargas

Organization and Program Overview

Organization

Launched as a free clinic in 1970, Venice Family Clinic (VFC) continues to be the first choice in affordable health care for low-income, uninsured and homeless families and individuals in the Venice Community. Now recognized as a Federally Qualified Health Center, VFC services as a medical home to over 26,000 patients and provides comprehensive primary care, specialty care, pediatrics, mental health, dental, and substance. As of 2018, VFC offers these services across twelve different sites in Venice, Santa Monica, Inglewood, and Culver City.

Program Introduction

The program that was evaluated during this project was Robert Levine Family Health Center's Teen Clinic. With multiple schools and community recreation centers within a three-mile radius of Levine,

VFC saw the need to have a clinic that was specifically geared towards health concerns of adolescent patients ages 12-25. Teen Clinic occurs in the afternoon on Monday, Tuesday and Wednesday of every week (although adolescent patients are seen any day/time of the week) and the clinical and office staff are trained and sensitive to the needs and confidentiality of adolescent concerns. The overarching purpose/goal of Teen Clinic is to allow a time (ages 12-25) for adolescent patients to mature in their understanding of their health/healthcare, social environment, and decision making while having a safe and confidential place to get their healthcare needs meet (a comprehensive list of Teen Clinics impacts are listed in Appendix I). Outside of general primary care, some additional health concerns include physicals and reproductive health care, diagnostic testing and medications, health education, mental health services, and weight management.

Evaluation Methodology

The aim of our evaluation was to see what kind and quality of impact Venice Family Clinic's Levine Teen Clinic program is having in the adolescent population in Venice. To understand this, we explored two broad research questions:

> ➢ What kind and quality of impact are we having on low-income adolescents in the Venice area?
> ➢ What aspects of our program are causing this impact?

Over the course of the project, we (a) developed and refined our ideas of intended impact and indicators, (b) designed and implemented a mixed methods outcome evaluation using both qualitative and quantitative means to collect and analyze data, (c) identified findings, and (d) considered the implications to those findings for program improvement and innovation.

This project began with a focus on the work of identifying and clarifying the intended impact of the Levine Teen Clinic program. Once the ideas of impact had been developed, we used the Heart Triangle™ model to identify qualitative and quantitative indicators of impact focused on the mental, behavioral and emotional changes in our adolescent patients that indicate we are achieving our impact. We then used these indicators to design a qualitative interview protocol land a quantitative questionnaire to measure our progress toward achieving our intended impact.

Qualitative Data Collection and Analysis

For the qualitative portion of the evaluation, we designed an in-depth interview protocol to gain data about the structural, qualitative changes resulting from our program. We used a convenience sampling technique to select active and willing participants, who represent the characteristics of the population we serve but may not be representative of our larger patient population (see Limitations section below). Our population size was 465. Our sample size was 19, and we drew our sample from the following strata of our population:

> ➤ Men and women from 12-25 years old
> ➤ Had at least three visits to Venice Family Clinic with one or more medical visits in the last year
> ➤ Primary language was English or Spanish

Our interview team consisted of three staff members and two experienced volunteers. Interviewers who did not participate in the Project Impact cohort meetings were trained in qualitative data collection and analysis prior to conducting interviews.

We then convened nineteen one-on-one interviews lasting from between 20 minutes and 45 minutes in length with a sample from the identified strata of the population. All patients interviewed voluntarily to do so and were not interviewed in the presence of their parents or guardians. The interviews were administered in person during the teen clinic in a private area.

Interviewers took notes during the interviews and filled in the notes immediately after the interview to obtain a substantive rendering of the interview.

We analyzed the data inductively using a modified version of thematic analysis. Interviewers implemented the first three phases of thematic analysis (becoming familiar with the data, generating initial codes and identifying themes) for each interview. The interviewers familiarized themselves with the data by reviewing the data from each interview four times, each time thinking through a different aspect of what the data reveal about the research question. The data were then bucketed into four categories to serve as an initial set of codes. Finally, initial themes were generated based on the pervasive insights from the data. This process allowed us to interpret the meaning and significance of the data from each interview.

Next, we brought all of the data analyses and initial themes together and implemented the next two phases of thematic analysis (reviewing themes, defining and naming themes). We reviewed the initial themes as a team to identify the overarching themes that emerged from the full scope of our data analysis to illuminate the collective insights and discoveries. We mapped these themes visually and examined them in various ways to gain a greater definition of the features of the themes, causes, and catalysts of the themes, new or surprising insights related to the themes, and relationships between the themes that were revealed in the data. We then determined the most significant and meaningful discoveries and brought them forward as findings to be described in the final phase of thematic analysis, this report.

Quantitative Data and Analysis

For the quantitative portion of the evaluation, we designed a questionnaire to collect data on our quantitative indicators of impact. We administered this instrument to 284 individuals and had a response of 52 (number of people who responded), an 18% response rate. The survey was administered over the phone to patients who agreed to answer the survey. Data collected over the phone were put directly into an electronic data collection tool by experienced volunteers.

The data were analyzed primarily using measures of central tendency. We identified key insights, patterns, and gaps within the data and incorporated these discoveries into the related findings. Pearson correlation was also used to determine links between questions.

The most significant discoveries from this evaluation are described in the findings that follow.

Limitations

We are aware that our sample may not be representative of our larger population.

Qualitative Data Limitations

To decrease respondent burden, we pulled our sample from adolescents who already had an appointment scheduled for Levine Teen Clinic during the interview period April 9-April 24, 2018. Interview respondents may differ from the larger population in a few ways. Interview respondents may be more engaged in Levine Teen Clinic services than the larger population. Participants may have more significant health problems than the larger population, assuming that patients who have had multiple visits correlate to the severity of their health problems.

Quantitative Data Limitations

Quantitative survey respondents were invited to participate via individual phone calls. Therefore, respondents may be more engaged with care, since they answered a phone call from Venice Family Clinic. There could be differences in patients who are easier to reach by phone, for example, it can be more difficult for patients experiencing homelessness to have a stable phone number.

Findings

Finding 1: Putting on the white coat

Key Insight: Teen patients seek to understand their health and put it into practice to have a healthier lifestyle

Description

When discussing the patient's role in their healthcare, most of our teen patients stated that they wanted to understand their health. When they step into the clinic room, they seek to acquire information about their bodies, their medical conditions, and steps they could take to improve their health. A patient said, "I think health is very important [and it is important] for a young person to know what's going on in your body." Teen patients discussed that they took proactive steps to learn about their health. As one patient mentioned, "I always have questions as to why this is happening or what is this pain over here and then… a simple solution or a simple answer. I'm like, oh that makes sense." Through our interviews, we came to realize that teen patients seek to have a comprehensive understanding of their health and are being vocal about it during their medical visits.

Through our interviews, it was also revealed that teen patients seek to learn about their health in order not to feel ignorant. One patient stated, "…Before coming here I've gone awhile without going to a doctor, so a ton of things have accumulated so when I got here I kept coming here regularly, it helped. I'm more aware of things and how it can affect other things in the body because everything is connected. I feel more educated cause I don't like to feel ignorant and I do not like not knowing things." Patients want to be equipped with knowledge in order to make educated decisions about their health. It is evident that teen patients realize the benefit of learning and feel empowered about their health. Our quantitative data reveal that 92% of patients reported that since coming to the teen clinic they have become more aware of how health and behavior are linked. It is evident through our quantitative data that our teen population are becoming knowledgeable as they continue to seek care at our teen clinic.

Figure 1. Since coming to teen clinic, I have become more aware of how health and behaviors are linked.

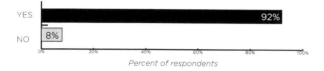

Our data reveal that patients use knowledge gained from teen clinic to inform their behaviors. One patient shared that because of her healthcare team's recommendation, she "used to eat lots of fast food and delivery, but now I cook more at home." Another patient said this about what she has learned from the teen clinic, "If there's a lot of sodium or that has a lot of sugar, I can [eat] this, but I have to have something to balance it... I'm more conscientious." Eighty-nine percent of patients surveyed agreed that since coming to the teen clinic, they have become more aware of how health and behaviors are linked. This is also reflected in their behaviors: 90% of survey respondents indicated that they devote time for self-care and that they consistently practice at least one healthy behavior weekly, with 27% of patients practicing 4+ healthy behaviors weekly.

We think there are a couple of different factors that could be contributing to this finding, though we did not specifically see these factors in our interviews. Parental support is a likely contributor to patients practicing healthy behavior. Some healthy behaviors require a change in habits, which is easier if family are supportive and willing to engage in these changes too. We were surprised to find that patients were so willing and able to take what they learned at the teen clinic and incorporate it into their lives.

Another contributing factor could be the delivery of health education services at the teen clinic. Patients may receive suggestions from providers that are then reinforced when they meet with health educators. Research calls this the "double knock," where the patient hears the same message from different staff. One could think that teens are not receptive to following orders for medical providers. We think that the way staff presents these messages to patients enables patients to be engaged, rather than turned off. As we mentioned in another finding, teen clinic patients crave knowledge and understanding. We think that patients are more receptive when provider instructions are explained, meaning that rather than the provider saying to the patient "get 30 minutes of exercise per day," the provider likely explains why this is important. We think that this more detailed explanation engages our teen patients who really want to understand. Additionally, we believe there may be some outside the clinic factors that are contributing to this, including research that younger generation (Gen Z) are more health conscious than other generations, specifically focusing more on preventive health behaviors.

Significance

It is great to observe that our teen patients are actively learning about their healthcare. It is commonly believed that teens tend to be uninterested or not completely engaged in their health. Based on our interviews it is significant to see that they are actually paying attention to the provider's recommendation and taking actions to remedy their health concerns. This is significant because patients use this knowledge to inform their decisions. Teen clinic patients are especially receptive to practicing preventive health measures, due to multiple factors. This is important because practicing healthy behaviors can prevent future health issues, allowing teens to live a healthier life in the future. By wanting to understand their bodies and their health, patients can make informed decisions about their health.

Recommendation

Over the course of the next year, we would like to maximize the clinic's teaching moments at patient's visit. This would include making sure we have a good learning environment where patients can learn.

Providers utilizing learning methods such as the teach-back method would enable them to assess the patient's understanding and mastery of the discussed health topic. This method would give insight into how well the provider explained or taught the information.

Finding 2: Adaptive "Morphin' time"
Key Insight: Teen patients tend to adapt to their clinical experience in order to get their healthcare needs met.

Description

Our data reveal that interviewees are adaptable in their healthcare environment. Based on our interviews, teen patients experienced some roadblocks when attempting to get their healthcare needs met. One of these roadblocks was poor communication between patient and provider. Teen patients reacted to these roadblocks by modifying how they approach their communication method. For example, one patient stated, "I find it hard to express what I want to say. Sometimes I feel embarrassed which is kind of hard. Being more vocal... I try to find a way to explain it if I don't know how to say it." This patient noticed that she was having difficulty communicating with her health provider. That led her to change the way she communicated with her healthcare team in order to get health needs met. Another patient stated, "Every time I come in I let them know the issues going on, and that's why I'm coming in more often. I still continue to let them know about the issue." This patient noticed that she was not being heard when she mentioned a health concern once. She learned that she had to state her issues more than once in order to get her healthcare needs met.

Another way teen patients are adapting in order to get their healthcare needs met is by relying on one of the patients' healthcare team. A patient expressed in one of our interviews that she was struggling to be heard by her provider to address her needs. This patient found resolution by being communicative with another member of her healthcare team. As the patient expressed, "Next time I came back, I made sure the nurse will help me. I will tell her kind of like everything that I want taken care of that day and then she kind of sorts it out for me after that." For this patient, the nurse was the team member the patient felt was attentive to her needs.

While we did not hear from our interviewees why certain members of their team were not meeting their needs, we suspect that the patient found it welcoming that the nurse heard her needs and took action to make the patient's request be met. Our quantitative data reflect that 98.1% of patients "very much" agreed that they felt that their health care team had their best interest at heart. It is satisfying to know that even though they have to be adaptive in how they communicate with their healthcare team, they are still able to either be more vocal or have someone in their healthcare team that listens to them.

Significance

Teen patients are conscientious of their environment and can adapt to it. Teen patients are able to detect whether or not they are being heard or acknowledged in their healthcare environment. They can discern who understands their needs and are able to take action to address them. We did not come across in our interviews how teen patients have this innate ability to adapt and get their needs met, but we are able to see they react to how the communication strength is to each one of them. It also gives insight that relationship and communication between the patient and the healthcare team need to improve. Not having a strong communication relationship with each of our patients hinders the clinic to fulfill its mission in providing quality primary health care to people in need. Teens evoked that they had challenges getting their health needs met due to challenging communication with their health care team. From interviewing our teen patients, it has informed us that we need to make improvement efforts in this population and possibly, to other populations we serve.

Recommendation

Over the course of next year, we would highly be recommended that providers and individuals in the healthcare team be retrained on effective communication skills including active listening. Such training will allow healthcare team members to build and foster a good relationship between staff and patients. Have a strong communication skill will allow the opportunity for patients to have an open and honest relationship with their healthcare team that will improve patient care and efficiency.

Finding 3: Which white coat?

Key Insight: Teen patients prefer to have a continuity of care with their primary care provider in order to have a strong clinical relationship.

Description

Our data reveal that strong relationships with providers are necessary to create a comfortable environment for teen patients to openly discuss their health concerns. Interviewees described the effective relationships with their providers as being able to see the same provider continuously, that know their medical history and feel comfortable speaking about any health concerns that they might have. What some of our teen patients are experiencing at our teen clinic is that they are not seeing the same provider for their medical visits. Instead, the patients are being seen by providers that have never met or have rarely seen.

One teen patient expressed her experience with continuity as "The more comfortable I get with the doctor, the easier it is to tell them what's wrong and what's going on than when you have someone that is kind of just reading off it, doesn't really know your situation, it's a little hard. You feel you can't really tell them anything because they aren't really understanding the way your doctor is understanding you." It is evident that teen patients are hesitant in discussing their health freely for fear that they will not be understood. This particular patient sensed the disconnection that was lacking and therefore did not obtain the optimum care that she previously had with her primary care provider. It has been

Based on the accounts of some of our teen patients, our resident providers have been viewed with more scrutiny compared to other providers. Being a teaching clinic, Venice family clinic collaborates with residency programs where residents are able to practice at some of our sites. From our interviews with our teen patients, they have less trust in them based on how they carried themselves. As one patient mentioned, "Sometimes they don't know kind of what they're… not that they don't know what they're doing, but it doesn't seem like they know you as well as your doctor knows you. It kind of throws you off a bit right there." The patient experienced a lack of connection with this resident provider while we didn't hear the reasons why this patient felt that disconnection, we assume that there was a lack of preparedness from the provider's end when the provider stepped into the room.

Even though our teen patients are highlighting the importance of continuity of care, it is reassuring to know that the majority of teen patients are still confident in talking to their health care team. Based on our surveys, 98.1 % of patients reported having more confidence in discussing health concerns since coming to our Venice Family Clinic. Although we are not certain what direct factors are contributing to this, we assume that the continuous presence of a strong healthcare team is allowing teen patients to have that confidence.

Figure 2. Through teen clinic I have more confidence in discussing my health concerns.

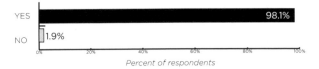

Percent of respondents

Significance

It is significant to note that teen patients want to develop strong relationships with their assigned provider. As a health organization, we want patients to feel comfortable and secure discussing their health concerns with their healthcare team. There have been multiple health sources including the American Academy of Family Practice; state that having continuity of care would result in a better standard of care. Therefore, it is important to note that in order to provide the best care and obtain better patient outcomes we need to improve our efforts and make sure that we are reaching it for all of our patients. In addition, we may need to retrain or provide the right tools to our resident providers to be more confident when stepping into the patient room.

Recommendation

Over the course of the year, we will continue to work on improving the continuity of care for our patients. We will retrain staff on emphasizing the importance of continuity of care and how to effectively schedule appointments with patient's assigned primary care physician. By improving the continuity of care for our patients, we will hope to reach better patient health outcomes and satisfaction. We would also recommend reinforcing the practice of care team model. Having a strong team between providers, nurses and medical assistants will make it possible to coordinate and accomplish patient's health needs.

Finding 4: Completing the Puzzle

Key insight: Patients understand mental health is an important part of overall health and wellbeing.

Description

When discussing health generally, patients brought up mental health as an important component of overall health. Even though the interview did not ask about mental health directly, patients spontaneously shared about their view of mental health as part of overall health. One patient said she wants to "be the best potential being that I can be physically, mentally, emotionally."

Our data reveal that interviewees were willing and open to sharing about their mental health. Patients talked about mental health the same way they talked about health in general. Since mental health is often stigmatized, we didn't expect patients to discuss it in our interviews. However, we found the opposite. Patients understand that participation in Venice Family Clinic's teen clinic includes more than just primary care- it also includes mental health. A patient shared that in order to be successful in the future "I need a good mental health state as well as a healthy body."

We suspect that teen clinic's integrated services either helps patients learn this integrated model of health and/or reinforces their existing understanding of mental health. Though we did not see this in the data, we think that the teen clinic's integrated model helped patients to see mental health as just another component of health. In the teen clinic, primary care staff administer mental health-related screenings to patients and discuss the results during the medical provider visit, including depression, domestic violence, and drug and alcohol use screenings. By identifying patients in primary care with mental health needs, patients may view this process as a regular part of primary care. These screenings are administered at the same time as general health screenings, such as obtaining vital signs. Patients who have been identified through the screenings as having mental health needs are connected to a therapist (who is on-call, often at the same site) on that same day, which could lead patients to think that discussing mental health concerns is a regular part of a primary care visit.

Significance

The lack of stigma seen in our data demonstrates that patients place the same value judgment on mental health as overall health. Patients are comfortable discussing mental health and view mental health as just another component of overall health. Patients view mental health needs as a need that can be met through the teen clinic. It shows that patients have a fuller view of what they consider to be healthy or not healthy. This finding leads us to believe that patients understand the mind-body connection and apply that model to their health. Gaining this perspective so early in life is a great benefit to our patients, as they can be more tuned-in to their health and mental health needs as they grow. This could cause patients to seek care more often and earlier-hence receiving early intervention to health issues before they get worse. By seeking care earlier, patients minimize the impact disease can have on their lives and saves the health care system money.

Finding 5: Adulting

Key insight: Teen clinic participants took ownership and responsibility for taking care of their health, reflecting a larger shift in responsibility for their overall health and wellness from the responsibility of the doctor to themselves.

Description

Teen clinic participants identified themselves as the most important part of their healthcare team. According to one patient interviewed, "I play the biggest role in my healthcare. My doctors are not going to force me to take medicine; I'm the one that has the obligation [to care for my health]." Interviewees understood that as young adults, they were responsible for participating in their health care. Older teen patients shared that they took over all responsibilities related to their healthcare (except possibly financial). An interviewee shared "It's been easy for me to communicate myself and make my own appointments rather than have my parents do it." Our quantitative data revealed that ninety-eight percent of survey respondents agreed that they have more confidence in discussing their health concerns since coming to the teen clinic.

The data showed that as patients have appointments at the teen clinic, they rely less on the doctor to "have all the answers" and more on themselves to understand what actions are needed in becoming a healthy individual. Data revealed that physicians recommended what treatment they may need, yet patients still had a sense of ownership and empowerment as to whether they followed the physician's recommendations. One patient stated, "A doctor can give me pills, but I know I have to make the decision to take them or not, I am the one affecting my own health."

Patients realized that they could control their health outcomes, as opposed to their health being determined by factors outside their control like their medical provider or genetics. The data reflected that patients felt they had the ability to impact their health. "I can take control of my health," said another patient. A patient expressed that if he doesn't "realiz[e] and acknowledge[e] my health, I can't seek the help that I want."

Though we did not hear this specifically in our interviews, we think that the teen clinic model of care may be empowering patients to take ownership of their health. Our quantitative survey data did show that 89% of patients surveyed agreed that their participation with their healthcare team has increased since coming to the teen clinic.

Figure 3. My participation with my Healhcare Team has increased since coming to Teen Clinic.

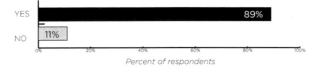

Percent of respondents

As mentioned in an earlier finding, the support that patients receive from teen clinic staff may be allowing them to take ownership of their health because the staff believes in them. Teens may feel more capable of successfully taking care of their health because of the emotional support provided by staff. Since the teen clinic is set up specifically for teens, staff set the expectation that the teen patient is the driver of their healthcare, even if a parent is present. By focusing on the patients' concerns (as opposed to the parents'), staff demonstrate to patients and parents that the teen is the primary focus.

Significance
Our findings reflect that teen clinic patients are taking ownership of their own health. They see and understand how their actions can

impact their health. They do not see the healthcare team as the driver of their health, but rather themselves. This acknowledgment of their significant role in their healthcare is surprising to us. We expected patients to identify external factors as contributors to their health, such as their healthcare team, parents, or forces beyond their control (genetic, social determinants of health). Owning their role in their health can lead patients to adopt healthy behaviors to prevent disease.

What we are seeing in the patients who attend teen clinic is a shift in mindset and practices in regard to decision making. Traditionally we rely on the doctor to make/inform all of our healthcare decisions and typically, without thinking, we follow their directive as we often think "the doctor knows best." It seems to be a generational shift in these adolescents to have the mindset of "I know best." It's also significant in that at a young age, these patients realize the importance of ownership and that they are in control. This is particularly an important trend to continue to notice and evaluate (in the healthcare field in general) as it seems to become harder and more time consuming to see your primary care physician.

Finding 6: The Cheerleader Effect
Key Insight: Patients were motivated by the support of their healthcare team to be responsible for their health and to prioritize their health.

Description
Teen clinic participants described that the support from their healthcare team motivated them to take ownership of their health and prioritize it. One patient shared this about their healthcare team "their concern for me helps me be more concerned about what I'm doing and [how I am] taking care of myself at home." The data revealed that the genuine support of their healthcare team catalyzed patients to continue working to improve their health. Another patient expressed "[there were] a lot of things I couldn't do before coming here... I'm glad that they got through to me."

In addition to patients feeling as though they have their healthcare teams support in healthy decision making, it appeared to be a theme that patients felt supported in their personal lives as well. A patient struggling from anorexia reports on how the staff has personally touched her: "They've played a huge role in helping me ... Because of them, I have been able to come out of a hole." This was seen on multiple occasions with many different patient's interviews—and patients are thankful for the consistency of support they receive at Teen Clinic. Looking at before and after coming to the teen clinic, data revealed that 90% of patients currently feel more supported by their healthcare team than they did before attending Teen Clinic.

Figure 4. Since coming to teen clinic, I feel more like my health care team has my best interests at heart.

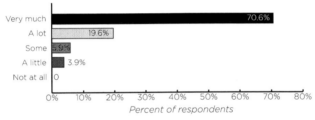

Ninety percent of patients reported that since coming to the teen clinic, they feel more like their health care team has their best interests at heart (see figure above). In our analysis, we found that feeling more like their health care team has their best interests at heart was statistically significantly correlated to seven other questions:

Table 1. Since coming to the teen clinic, I feel more like my health care team has my best interests at heart.

Correlated Survey Questions	Pearson Correlation	Significance (2-tailed)	N
Do you feel like you can rely on your healthcare team more now than you did before coming to the teen clinic?	.325*	.21	50
Through teen clinic, I have more confidence in discussing my health concerns.	.470**	.001	51

Correlated Survey Questions	Pearson Correlation	Significance (2-tailed)	N
Since coming to the teen clinic, I have become more aware of how health and behaviors are linked.	.309*	.027	51
Since coming to the teen clinic, I devote time for self-care.	.403**	.003	51
On a scale of 1-5 where 1 means not at all and 5 means very much, how much has your understanding of your health improved since coming to the teen clinic?	.481**	.0	51
I feel more confident that I am getting my healthcare needs met at the teen clinic.	.521**	.0	51
How much more confident are you in your ability to integrate healthy behaviors into your daily life?	.373**	.007	51

Significance

It is important to note the significance of patients feeling supported by their healthcare team leads to healthy behavior change, but also the impact that the Levine staff is having on our patients and their lives go well beyond giving medical advice. The healthcare system has so many demands on productivity, cycle times and being efficient, it can be hard to be able to connect on a deeper level, to truly understand them holistically, and have an opportunity to be a positive influence. Our staff at Levine, through this analysis, has shown that they foster an environment of support and being effective not only as healthcare practitioners but individuals attending to the social needs of the community they serve. Also important is that when patients feel more supported, that their health care team cares about them, this can lead to more engagement in their health care and even potentially impact practicing healthy behaviors.

Finding 7: Back to the Future

Key Insight: Patient's experiences at VFC has helped shape aspirations for the patient's future.

Description

Regardless of positive or negative experiences of being a patient at VFC, patients were very clear about how their engagements at Teen Clinic have helped shaped their vision of their career path. Patients who have expressed having positive experiences want to work in service because they were deeply and positively affected; those patients who have had more negative experiences wanted to work in service to help others avoid similar issues they endured. A patient stated, "I also talked to them that and said I want to be a doctor, they gave me suggestions, support and they helped me. The support here has been a big thing. I get support, be helped, and not be judged."

Along with the Teen Clinic staff being influential on patient's aspirations of having a career in and being successful in social and medical services, it was communicated that having a successful career and future is encompassing of being a healthy individual. Just as having a successful career (particularly in healthcare) is a process, takes time, many interventions, just as the steps each needs to take to become and/or maintain being a healthy individual.

Data revealed that patients understood the connection between being health/creating healthy habits help facilitate having a healthy career. When patients were asked about their life in 5 years, one individual stated, "Just prospering in whatever I do. Being healthy and happy and conscious about it at the same time..." Many patients talked about the importance of taking steps to remain healthy in the upcoming years, and it was a theme to see that part of having a fulfilling future is being a healthy individual in their current state.

Significance

In working with teens and adolescents, we expected to hear about how their social circles and networks have an impact on their potential career. However, it was also clear that at this stage, VFC staff have a much larger impact in influencing patients' career goals of working in service/healthcare and being able to connect being a healthy individual to a healthy career. Since coming to the teen clinic, about 46 of 51 of patient's survey stated they are much more devoted to living a healthy future.

Figure 5. How much more devoted are you to living a healthy future?

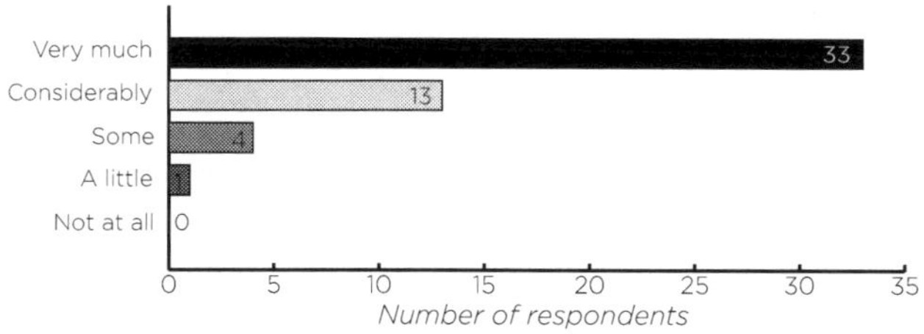

Seen through the responses of these interviews, it remains consistent that our adolescent patients are having a positive and meaningful response to our healthcare providers at Teen Clinic. It is also amazing to find how influential the clinical staff, but even more so, at a young age, these patients can connect how being healthy and a successful career coincide. Often, we as healthcare providers are the front line for the most up to date medical information; and learning that our adolescent patients can connect being/maintaining being healthy should be inspiring that patients are applying what is being learned in the exam room. It is clear to see here that we, as health care professionals, play a much more influential role in a patient's life outside of being just their doctor, nurse, MA, etc.

Recommendations

It has been wonderful to hear that the staff has engaged the patients beyond their aspirations of being healthy individuals but in their future career goals. To continue to engage the patients in this manner, it is recommended that at some points in the year, to have a patient board that may ask them questions such as "in 5 years I want to be…" or "my health goals for the future are…" We can continue to pay attention to patient goals and utilize them as an intervention to educate and connect things back to being healthy individuals.

Conclusion: Waiting on the World to Change

The data revealed that Teen Clinic patients have experience a number of shifts in both their perspectives and their behavior related to their health. Along with this, there is also evidence of a personal shift from traditional medicine to a more revolutionary approach.

In a much broader spectrum of this data, we are seeing elements of a shift on how healthcare is delivered and what is encompassing of the definition of healthcare. Data revealed a more holistic approach to healthcare, such as assistance with applying/understanding individual's health insurance, incorporating an interdisciplinary/ collaborative care model and empowering the individual patient to participate in their health and assimilate information learned. Data also reveal the shift of patients being more assertive in prioritizing their health, mental health, incorporating preventative care into their lifestyle, understanding what it takes to be dedicated to become healthier and/or maintain a healthy lifestyle and future.

In academia, it often takes years, sometimes decades, to see what interventions work and on such a large scale. As the healthcare field moves towards being preventative vs. reactionary, there is evidence that this model is of great value to the healthcare system and the consumer at Teen Clinic. Data show that patients in Teen Clinic have an understanding of the importance of preventative care as well as practicing preventative care. One patient explained his understanding of the importance of preventative care as gaining knowledge: "I go to the doctors, I am always interested in my health to try to get as much info as possible to better myself and prevent illness." The practice of preventative care is, of course, practiced differently with different patients and for various reasons. However, one patient stated, "Since

I know it's hard to get appointments, I do healthier activities for my mental and physical health." Self-care is an example of a preventative intervention that patients complete outside the clinical walls and over 90% of adolescent patients surveyed reported they have started to incorporate self-care into their lives since attending Teen Clinic.

Figure 6. Since Coming to Teen Clinic
I Devote Time for Self Care

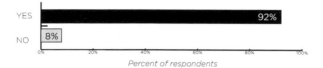

Percent of respondents

These young patients have a great understanding of and are taking action in preventative healthcare. Traditionally healthcare is reactionary vs. preventative, and there is a huge significance of Teen Clinic being able to instill those elements into their patients. Being that these practices continue into these patient's adulthood, and the element of preventative care can be conveyed to the broader population, we at VFC/Teen Clinic can start to see an increasingly healthier community.

The other significance of incorporating different elements into delivering healthcare is that not only are patients being treated for their physical health (traditional medicine) patients are getting holistic treatment (a more revolutionary approach to medicine). Knowing and hearing that patients are having a meaningful experience/reaction to these different elements is justification that Teen Clinic is meeting the needs of its community.

While understanding the influence VFC Staff on patients at Teen Clinic, it is recommended that VFC continue to assess patients with PRAPARE (social determinants of health) to see what other needs we could potentially address in the clinical setting when looking to address the results of the PRAPARE Assessment that allows VFC departments to collaborate as well as implement interventions for patients to attend.

Words Alive

Words Alive Westreich Scholarship

Amanda Birmingham Bonds, Jessica Fryman
Sara Mortensen, Patrick Stewart

About the Organization: Words Alive

The purpose of this report is to present the process Words Alive undertook, and the findings discovered, as we set out to measure the impact of our Words Alive Westreich Scholarship program.

Established in 1999, Words Alive was founded on the belief that if you value reading and understand its fundamental connection to all aspects of your life, you will thrive as a lifelong learner — ready to transform your community. In that vein, our mission is to open opportunities for life success by inspiring a commitment to reading, and with our three primary programs: Read Aloud, Teen Services and Family Literacy, Words Alive provides life-changing services to more than 3,800 underserved students and families throughout Southern California monthly.

About the Program: Words Alive Westreich Scholarship

Founded by philanthropist Ruth Westreich in 2007, the Words Alive Westreich Scholarship (WAWS) aims to support graduates of the Juvenile Court and Community Schools district as they work to achieve their higher education goals at the college or vocational level. All participating scholars have faced extraordinary circumstances such as homelessness, exposure to gang violence, struggles with alcohol/drug abuse, teen pregnancy or impact by the justice system.

Disbursed in monthly stipends to their personal checking account, the financial award can be used to cover living expenses such as rent, utilities, food, basic toiletries, public transportation, and child care. Additionally, the program pairs recipients with a mentor. Through the mentorship, students have individualized support navigating the college landscape from a career professional, gain assistance in accessing academic and community resources, learn relationship-building skills, and often, find a friendly shoulder to lean on. The WAWS program also offers personal and professional development opportunities through group workshops on many topics including financial literacy, resume building, job interviewing skills and time management.

Evaluation Methodology

To continually provide meaningful and evaluation-driven programming, Word Alive commenced the seven-month Project Impact with Dialogues in Action (DIA) project to analyze the impact of our Words Alive Westreich Scholarship program using a mixed method qualitative and quantitative evaluation model. Through this process, we had an opportunity to view our program through the lens of the scholarship recipients, past and present, and their mentors to determine opportunities to enhance our program delivery.

The aim of our evaluation was to ascertain the type of impact our program has on the Words Alive Westreich Scholarship recipients. Over the course of seven months, our team developed and refined ideas of intended impact and indicators and designed and implemented both qualitative and quantitative means to collect and analyze data.

Qualitative Data Collection and Analysis

For the qualitative portion of the evaluation, we designed an in-depth interview protocol to gain data about the structural, qualitative changes resulting from our program. We used a purposeful stratified sampling technique to select a representative sample from the population we serve. Our population size was 39 scholars. Our sample size was 9 and we drew our sample from the following strata of our population:

> ➢ Current and former scholars and mentors who had participated in the program between fall 2012-spring 2018
> ➢ Scholars who attended university locally and those who attended schools outside of San Diego and therefore had long-distance mentorships
> ➢ Amount of scholarship funding received

We also interviewed six mentors who worked with students locally and remotely across several program years. Many of the mentors we interviewed had mentored more than one scholar through the years and could compare those experiences.

We then convened one-on-one interviews lasting from between 45 minutes and one hour in length with a sample from the identified strata of the population. Interviewers took notes during the interviews and filled in the notes immediately after the interview to obtain a substantive rendering of the interview.

We analyzed the data inductively using a modified version of thematic analysis. Interviewers implemented the first three phases of thematic analysis (becoming familiar with the data, generating initial codes and identifying themes) for each interview. The interviewers familiarized themselves with the data by reviewing the data from each interview four times, each time thinking through a different aspect of what the data reveal about the research question. The data were then bucketed into four categories to serve as an initial set of codes. Finally, initial themes were generated based on the pervasive insights from the data. This process allowed us to interpret the meaning and significance of the data from each interview.

Next, we brought all of the data analyses and initial themes together and implemented the next two phases of thematic analysis (reviewing themes, defining and naming themes). We reviewed the initial themes as a team to identify the overarching themes that emerged from the full scope of our data analysis to illuminate the collective insights and discoveries. We mapped these themes visually and examined them in various ways to gain greater definition of the features of the themes, causes and catalysts of the themes, new or surprising insights related to the themes, and relationships between the themes that were revealed in the data. We then determined the most significant and meaningful discoveries and brought them forward as findings to be described in the final phase of thematic analysis, this report.

Quantitative Data and Analysis

For the quantitative portion of the evaluation, we designed a questionnaire to collect data on our quantitative indicators of impact. We administered this instrument to 39 scholars (the entire population of scholars) and had a response of 13, a 33% response rate. The data were analyzed primarily using measures of central tendency. We identified key insights, patterns, and gaps within the data and incorporated these discoveries into the related findings.

We detail our findings below. When quoting from our interviews, we indicate whether the quote is from a scholar or a mentor.

Findings

Finding #1 – More Than Money: Learning From and Limitations Of Financial Awards

One might assume that the most impactful element of a scholarship program would be the money itself. However, our research found that the money awarded through the scholarship was not enough to negate the broader constraints of scholars' financial circumstances nor to ensure a sense of financial security. That being said, a much-welcomed finding is that, as a group, scholars are thinking about and using money differently than they did before the program.

The scholarship program has several features intended to help students develop positive financial habits and feel more financially secure. Unlike many traditional scholarship programs, students can spend their awarded funds on living expenses such as rent, food, public transportation and child care. Money is disbursed monthly into personal checking accounts for greater access to cover these kinds of off-campus expenses and is often a student's first time establishing a relationship with a bank. Additionally, students attend a financial literacy course led by experts in the field and are encouraged to work with their mentor on budgeting practices throughout the year.

Interviews with scholars who attended the workshop and/or addressed budgeting with their mentor described a better understanding of spending behaviors and different decision making about how to use their money.

About understanding their spending behavior, scholars said:

> [The financial workshop] made me realize how much I was wasting and how much I accumulate each month by going to restaurants instead of eating at home. – *Scholar, age 22*

> I've been using a template that my mentor shared with me. I ask myself, 'Do I really need this? Do I want to waste my money on this? Have I bought the right things first?' I'm more aware of what I buy...For example, do I want to go to Jack in the Box and feed myself for an hour or go to the grocery store and feed myself for a week. – *Scholar, age 26*

About making money decisions differently, many scholars reported saving money for the first time in their lives, while others described strategizing their spending in other ways:

> I'm spending more of my money on school supplies and using free school resources for food. I'm saving scholarships for

further down the line. I'm using that money for other materials, like in 1-2 years when I know I'll have like a $5,000 tuition. So, I'm planning for that...I'm stretching my budgets to cover everything I need. I'll spend 3 days researching something I need to buy to find the best price. I think these changes are feeding my motivation and keeping it alive. – *Scholar, age 20*

When I first got the scholarship, I was going through a tough time. I had just been kicked out of my living situation and I was living off the scholarship money. So, I learned how to budget money for necessities like food. I had my young daughter, so I had to think about her. I didn't really have help, so I had to figure it out on my own and I was very young. This taught me how to save money and not spend on things you don't need. And the scholarship money was limited so I learned how to extend it out. – *Scholar, age 18*

Figure 1. Percent of Scholars Who Reported
Often or Always Using Budgeting Skills and Tools

Survey responses reflected a similar sentiment, in which after participating in the program, 81% scholars reported that they often or always use budgeting skills and tools to manage their financial situation than reported doing so before participating in the program.

It wasn't easy though, and in their eyes, consistency and discipline with budgeting remains a challenge:

I go on and off with the financial habits. I try to tell myself, it's okay just keep it in your head. I have done better budgeting in the past, but then I have an emotional breakdown and that makes all the habits go away. I want to get back to it...I just need more practice with budgeting. – Scholar, age 22

My [money] management fluctuates. I set up a savings account at a different bank not tied to the app on my phone where I can transfer money between accounts easily, and I didn't get the card. That way I have to make a special trip to the bank to take the money out, which I know I wouldn't want to do. I'll save up a lot, like $500 until recently, but then I'll dip into it for some expense and have to build it back up. Now I have $260+ in that account and I know I have to get back on track and not touch it. – *Scholar, age 26*

We believe a contributing factor to success with budding budgeting skills may be the amount of money awarded to scholars. All scholars participating in the program have been impacted by extraordinary life circumstances and the financial hardship connected to those circumstances, and there was consensus among interviewed scholars that the amount of their financial award was not significant enough to cause lasting financial change or relief in the larger context of their lives. However, seen in the chart below, students who received larger financial awards reported feeling less stressed about their financial situation, as well as sticking to their personal budget and accessing financial resources outside their scholarship more often.

Figure 2. Scholar Financial Management as Compared by Size of Awarded Scholarship Funds

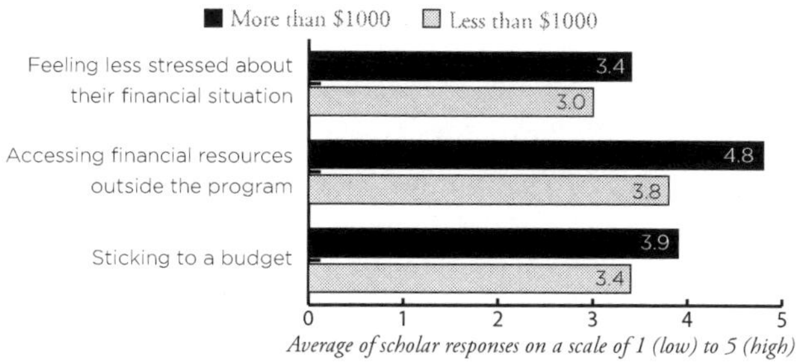

■ More than $1000   ☐ Less than $1000

Feeling less stressed about their financial situation	3.4 / 3.0
Accessing financial resources outside the program	4.8 / 3.8
Sticking to a budget	3.9 / 3.4

Average of scholar responses on a scale of 1 (low) to 5 (high)

Significance

A central goal of the WAWS program is to provide funding to support a scholar's academic trajectory. That the financial component is not restricted to certain kinds of expenses makes the scholarship both unique and a powerful tool to address the "real life" financial obstacles that keep scholars from focusing on their education. As it stands, scholarship awards are not enough to remove those obstacles completely. An intended impact for this program is that scholars work toward a level of financial sustainability by building positive financial habits. As one mentor put it, "any new financial habits are a big deal" and while not perfect in execution, new understanding and practices are in fact taking hold and endowing scholars with a new skillset for managing their challenging financial situations to leverage the resources they have.

One scholar summarized this reality beautifully: "I have more common sense, better decision-making skills and am wiser. Financial burden takes a lot out of you, [but] I don't feel as dragged down by it." – *Scholar, age 20*

Possible Responses
> Award more money per student to further ease financial strain.
> Ensure mentors attend the group financial literacy workshop, so they are equipped to assist students throughout the year.
> Offer 1:1 financial conferencing with experts in the field beyond or in place of a "one-size-fits-all" workshop.

As we dove into student interviews and survey responses we concluded that skills of leveraging the money they received as part of the scholarship outlasted the money itself, and that scholars who reported these skills gained them by adhering to program requirements and utilizing the mentorship pillar of the program. As a trend discussed in the findings that follow, scholars who met with their mentor consistently, often and face-to-face benefited most.

Finding #2 – Raising the Bar: Communicated Expectations
Improve Student Performance

Remaining eligible for the WAWS program requires that students regularly meet with their mentor, turn in academic progress reports, maintain a 2.0 GPA while enrolled in six credits and attend at least three of the professional development workshops offered throughout the program year. The program was intentionally designed with these requirements with the hope that students would develop habits of accountability and timely communication. We also hope that students will learn that they will face consequences if they do not complete program requirements in a timely manner. For example, a late fund request could result in not receiving their financial aid until the next month, or if a student does not attend the required number of workshops, they could lose eligibility for the scholarship for the next school year.

Through the interviews, we found that many students did, in fact, learn these skills. One scholar said very explicitly:

> I've learned to have more responsibility. There are different tasks we have to do to complete the scholarship, like submitting our grades and meeting with our mentor once a month. We have to write notes about what happened during the month. This responsibility I've learned also helps a lot in school and with my job. – *Scholar, age 23*

Another scholar remarked:

> I've learned how to be on top of things, how to make deadlines and turn things in on time. It's been good practice. – *Scholar, age 22*

Yet another scholar said:

> "The number one and most valuable thing I've learned is organization. To get the funds you're being checked in on monthly and that forced me to change my life around and make education my number one priority." – *Scholar, age 25*

Clearly, the program requirements had the impact we intended. These requirements held students accountable and forced them to stay engaged with the program, and in the process, they learned responsibility, increased their communication skills and prioritized the scholarship and their education.

However, we also found that these requirements only had the impact we intended if the scholars understood and perceived them as mandatory. This past year it became clear to us that one scholar, who only met with his mentor three times, didn't understand that attending the workshops was a mandatory requirement of the program.

In the survey, this scholar responded "moderately" to the statement: "I know what is expected of me by Words Alive and my mentor." In this scholar's interview, we saw a general lack of benefit from the WAWS program. When asked, "What changes are you seeing in your life as a result of the program?" he responded, "I haven't really seen any changes in my life." Comparing this answer with the other scholars, we see how the requirements being mandatory is absolutely essential.

Significance

It is significant that many scholars mentioned that the skills they learned because of these program requirements were then applied to other aspects of their life, such as school and work, which is imperative on their journey to adulthood.

We also found it interesting and surprising that while many scholars stated they had learned these skills (i.e. timely email communication, responsibility, organization, time management, etc.), they also often cited these same skills when asked about the recurring challenges they face. This points to the fact that these skills are a work in progress and take years to develop. The scholars' self-awareness in their development is important because it shows they are capable of realizing where they started, what they have learned from the program and where they still have room for improvement.

Possible Responses
> Modify the program requirements so that the mentors have more structure and requirements.
> Implement stricter, more immediate consequences for scholars when they fail to meet a requirement.
> Emphasize communication about what is mandatory and what is not. Update Terms & Conditions of the program to include a schedule of deadlines and clear communication about what is mandatory, and have scholars sign it at the orientation.
> Standardize financial award amounts. All scholars have the same requirements, so the reward should be the same too.
> Encourage students to find a mentor outside of the WAWS program.

Finding #3 – Consistent Mentoring Inspires Consistent Students

Historically, the first-year scholarship students don't answer emails, show up late, if at all, miss important deadlines and struggle to follow up when they say they will. Few offer excuses or apologies because before they entered the program, they were not accustomed to being asked for an explanation.

Interviews with scholars, all graduates of alternative high schools, revealed that they were unprepared for what would be expected of them in college and "the real world." But through the norms and expectations of the WAWS program, scholars start to realize what is expected of them in the program, in school, future jobs and in healthy adult relationships.

About communicating violated expectations, one mentor said:

I tried to be direct and honest. When my [first-year mentee] stood me up once or twice, I wrote her a letter and sent it to her home, telling her my expectations and how she had let me down. I hope she has a better idea that you have to show up and that commitments mean something.

Scholars who met with their mentor consistently, on the other hand, demonstrated how that consistency became part of how they operated. This was especially true for scholars who had multi-year experiences in the program.

One such scholar, who now works as a financial advisor and manages a small group of employees, attributed her leadership skills to her mentor's consistency:

> [My mentor] would visit me at school. We kept in contact and would catch up often, we would go hiking or meet up to eat. She was a really good friend," the scholar said. "[She] taught me what it meant to be consistent. – *Scholar, age 18*

Another scholar went on to say: "[My mentor] keeps me on track and helps me think of how to tackle things – usually along the lines of 'stay on top of that until it's done,'" listing actions she's taken as a result: consistently visiting professors during office hours to ask for grade progress or get help and following up by phone if an email goes unanswered. "I'm adulting way better because of these skills." – Scholar, age 26

When consistency in relationships becomes a habit, it bleeds into other aspects of life. Our research shows scholars with consistent mentorship also study regularly, turn in assignments on time and pay their bills when they are due.

One hundred percent of the scholars surveyed said they now take advantage of academic, professional and community resources at their disposal. Again, students who met with their mentor more frequently reported better follow through and higher competencies in several skillsets as demonstrated in the graph below.

see chart on next page

Significance

The lives of most scholars up to the point of participating in the program have been anything but consistent. Their parents have been

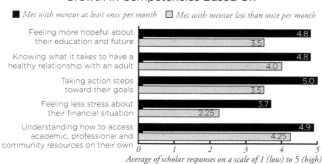

Figure 3. Comparison Of Students' Self-reported
Growth In Competencies Based On

■ *Met with mentor at least once per month*   ☐ *Met with mentor less than once per month*

Feeling more hopeful about their education and future: 4.8 / 3.5
Knowing what it takes to have a healthy relationship with an adult: 4.8 / 4.0
Taking action steps toward their goals: 5.0 / 3.5
Feeling less stress about their financial situation: 3.7 / 2.25
Understanding how to access academic, professional and community resources on their own: 4.9 / 4.25

Average of scholar responses on a scale of 1 (low) to 5 (high)

in and out of jail, in and out of drug rehab centers – and essentially, in and out of their lives. At times, the scholars have been unsure where they will sleep on any given night or when they will eat their next meal. Surviving one day to the next is all they know.

But when an engaged Words Alive mentor enters the picture, it gives the scholar new context for what it means to be reliable, to be professional, to be a successful adult. Like all skills – consistency is a learned behavior. Mentors who consistently interact with the scholars keep them accountable to the requirements of their schools, the scholarship program and their goals.

Possible Responses

➤ Implement a mentorship log for mentors and their scholars to track their conversations and what needs to be followed up on for each meeting.

➤ Require mentors to attend the scholars' workshops so mentors can ensure knowledge learned is applied.

➤ Mentors attend quarterly mentor-only meetings for additional training opportunities, roundtable discussions, etc.

Finding #4 – Face-to-Face: Facetime With Mentors Means Stronger Rapport, Greater Success

Through interviews with both students and mentors, we found

that mentorship was key to success for the scholars in the program. Scholars who reported a close bond with their mentor, established through frequent meetings, not only were more likely to follow through on their mentor's advice but also felt like they weren't "alone."

Conversely, students with long-distance mentors struggled to form an attachment to them. Scholars and mentors alike reported awkward Skype interactions and missed phone calls. Simply put: Without having to look someone in the eye, it's easier to flake. These factors made it difficult to build rapport, resulting in relationships that hinged solely on obligation.

"I think it would definitely be easier if it was a closer distance. We're mostly limited to phone calls," one mentor said. "When she is in town, it's often pretty brief but I think our interactions go better in person."

One pair built a strong rapport despite the distance. The difference? They were able to meet in-person when possible:

> [My mentor] would go above and beyond to meet me where I was at. If we were meeting, she would come to me a lot of times. She would take trips to San Francisco to visit her niece and then stop by and see me. Having her support made the biggest difference. My parents couldn't come visit me, but she did – and it was such a comfort. – *Scholar, age 24*

Significance

Trust is the fundamental building block of all successful relationships – and the mentor/mentee relationship is no different. But trust is built over time and difficult to establish in a phone call. Without that element of trust and essentially, rapport, mentees have difficulty opening up, asking for help or placing value on the resources offered. On the flip side, mentors feel like they are prying or stepping out of bounds when trying to follow up or hold their mentee accountable.

This finding indicated that impactful mentorships underwent a period of relationship-building first – and that happens best face-to-face.

Possible Responses
> New scholars in the program must live and attend school in San Diego during their first year in the scholarship program.
> Recruit mentors in the cities where students attend school and offer them webinar training.

Finding #5 – "I feel like a better person. I feel so free."
While the intended impacts of the program included relationship-building with others, one surprising result discovered during this study was participants' changing relationship with themselves.

Through their scholarship application essays and interviews for this study, most if not all, of the students discussed the trauma in their lives. It's no secret that an unstable childhood can contribute to unhealthy personal relationships in adulthood. Many of the students revealed abusive romantic partners, the inability to enforce boundaries with their family members and feelings of isolation from peers who couldn't relate.

However, through a consistent relationship with their mentor as described in Finding #3 and the support of their WAWS cohort as described in Finding #6, students developed and employed healthy relationship skills with others. According to this study, 85% of scholars surveyed said they felt more confident in putting healthy relationship skills into action. For one scholar, healthy relationship skills meant establishing and exercising new boundaries: "I've learned to say no to certain people."

This new-found confidence coupled with realizing the value of healthy relationships, networking, community engagement and mentorship, led to many students and their mentors saying that the students simply found themselves much more open to communication after participating in the program.

One mentor described this growth in her mentee as: "She does a good job at assessing people and choosing to be with people who are good examples. She has become very open with me."

Perhaps even more impactful, however, was the growth scholars recognized within themselves. Many students initially felt trapped by the labels placed on them by society: at-risk, homeless, teen parent, juvenile delinquent. Before their participation in the program, many said they never thought they could go to college. In survey responses, they described themselves as "troubled, scared, lazy, unmotivated, unprepared and unfocused" before participating in the program.

But after at least a year in the program, they became scholars – describing themselves instead with more positive terms such as "responsible, confident, passionate, ready and focused."

In-line with these terms alluding to a new sense of agency, scholars described taking action:

> I believe that I'm smart enough to accomplish my goals. I believe I'm capable of taking actions to make changes, that I can identify those actions, and make the changes. Most importantly, I believe in myself, that I'm the only person who can do this. I've learned to identify what the challenges are and be specific as you can be to make that challenge a goal, to make it a positive. – *Scholar, age 25*

> I take action, go out and get the things that are beneficial for me instead of waiting for them to come to me. – *Scholar, age 26*

For many program participants, that shift stems from the support of their mentor and Words Alive staff. In interviews with scholars, they said that having someone cheer them on made them not want to give up, helped them realize they could rise above their circumstances and see themselves as more capable!

One scholar said:

> I've grown so much. I appreciate hearing the uplifting things [my mentor and Words Alive staff] say. It helps me remember my accomplishments and not just my struggles. I feel like a better person; I feel so free. – *Scholar, age 26*

Another scholar shared:

> I've learned self-care, self-love and self-respect...with self-love, especially when you have so many obstacles, helps everything else. Before I didn't know any better. I'm pushing myself to ask questions and see how much I've accomplished. I'm reclaiming my identity as a teen mom, as undocumented. Before, I didn't love myself, I just saw the labels society threw at me, like screw-up, outlaw, rebel and minority. I didn't like waking up to that.
> – *Scholar, age 25*

With a redefined, positive perspective of themselves and skills honed to address their circumstances, 100% of students surveyed said the program helped them feel at least moderately more in control of their choices.

Figure 4. Average student response for indicators of self-confidence

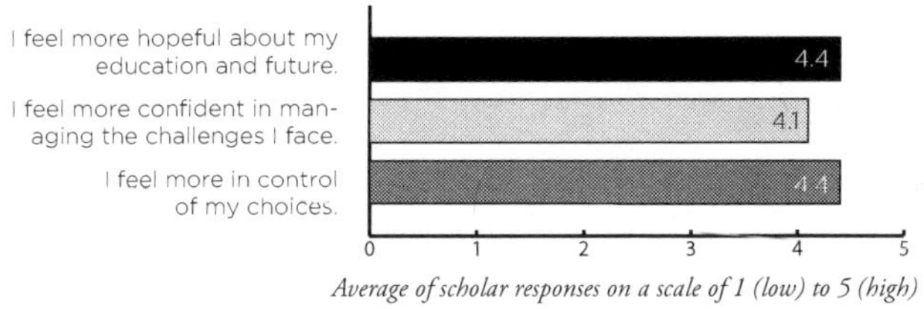

Average of scholar responses on a scale of 1 (low) to 5 (high)

To love oneself – to truly feel confident both in and out of one's skin – is important if one is to break free from the trappings of harmful and limiting environments. That the program scholars develop that confidence in such dramatic ways is remarkable. As one scholar shared, "I'm more positive about everything and learned to appreciate myself more. I wish I had a friend like me." – Scholar, age 26

Significance

Focused on the expectations and labels placed on them by society, students often say they never imagined they would graduate high school let alone go to college. But as students are repeatedly and genuinely told, "you can do it," our findings indicate they begin to believe it. This confidence translates to several other attributes, such as motivation and resilience, that help drive scholars' success.

Equally, one's desire to cultivate new relationships, create a personal goal of helping others, and confidently navigate the world fosters new opportunities. Being able to identify and develop in these two areas and recognize their importance will provide lasting positive impact.

Possible Responses

➤ Mentors and staff become more participatory in scholars' lives (attend graduations and other ceremonies, sporting events if the student is an athlete, etc.).

➤ Program staff to regularly remind mentors to send words of encouragement to their mentees.

➤ Program staff to send birthday cards and other celebratory communication when appropriate.

➤ Continue to diversify learning opportunities for scholars, not only through new workshop opportunities but other cultural opportunities.

Finding #6 – Better Together: Becoming Aware of Peer Relationships

The WAWS program also opportunities for scholars to participate in group activities in order to make deeper connections within their cohort and experience new things in the community. These activities, beyond the mandated workshop participation, include volunteerism, meal-sharing, outings to sporting events or performing arts shows and an extension of the Adolescent Book Group designed specifically for them.

As scholars begin to experience new environments, they find that their personal backgrounds can be dramatically different from many of their peers, making a sense of "belonging" and connection with others difficult. However, by spending time with one another during designed activities in the program, scholars got to know each other better, and in time, relate. Many of the students participating in the program recognized an elevated awareness of the peer relationships within the group – other young people who have shared experiences and whose camaraderie can provide a sense of safety and mutual well-being.

"I didn't realize before, how many kids were in situations similar to me," said one current participant. Finding common ground with her program peers helped her reach out at school: "I found a society oriented towards youth in foster care, homeless, orphaned or in other difficult situations or for kids whose parents weren't emotionally available. I became involved in the society and got another scholarship through them," she continued. (Scholar, age 24)

In addition to developing like-minded peer relationships within the WAWS group, and then feeling confident to seek out those relationships and support systems beyond the group, the students also expressed an increased level of "community engagement" – a new level of ease with networking, finding resources, giving back and being a resource for each other.

> I like to talk with my classmates and have little conversations. Through small talk I found out that one of my classmate's boyfriend was mistreating her. I encouraged her by sharing my past and my experience with domestic violence. I suggested she go to a therapist and even suggested I could go with her if she [needed the] support. – *Scholar, age 22*

Significance

No one wants to feel alone, that their experiences, especially traumatic, are isolated, or that no one else understands their path. That the WAWS program is designed to meet the needs of students and young people sharing very particular and specific backgrounds is unique, and on one that the students clearly have been able to capitalize. Additionally, as the young people who participate in the program progress, they have found it not only helpful to their peers, but also beneficial to themselves, to be able to recognize the value of these peer relationships and both use them to seek assistance and provide leadership when appropriate.

Possible Responses

➤ Offer more social group outings such as sporting events, performing arts shows or potlucks.

➤ Provide networking opportunities with other peer groups who have similar shared experiences and backgrounds.

➤ Create an online social network system for connections in and out of WAWS with the ability to share personal and professional connections and resources for growth and development.

Finding #7 – The Mentee Becomes the Mentor

We were surprised to find that through participating in the program and developing a relationship with their mentors, our scholars in turn became mentors for their peers.

When asked what they were passionate about, six out of nine of the scholars interviewed said "helping people." Many of the scholars are pursuing careers such as social work, therapy, and child development with the ultimate goal of helping youth that have similar stories to their own.

In addition, many of the scholars spoke directly about becoming mentors for their peers. One scholar said:

> Now, I pass on the advice my mentors have given me to other people. I'm a mentor for some of the students at Lindsay because I've been in their shoes. It's good to share your experience because they can see a role model and can relate to you. It gives them faith that things will work out… I just try to be a helping person and when someone's experiencing a lot of emotions I try to be a calming presence like the calming presence my mentors

have been for me. I've learned to ask for help and people still ask me for help. – *Scholar, age 22*

It's clear from this example and others that being a mentor wasn't necessarily an innate skill the scholars possessed, but something they learned through their relationship with their WAWS mentor. This statement from one of our scholars illustrates the range of skills these students learned from their mentors:

> I valued [my mentor's] honesty. She would be upfront but in a professional way. I learned how to be that way with other people. 'Let's go grab coffee' is not something I had done before but now do with other people. – *Scholar, age 24*

Significance

One of our intended impacts for this program is that scholars form healthy and meaningful relationships with their peers and adults. Because of their upbringing, many of our scholars lack healthy adult relationships in their lives. To see the students develop relationship-building skills and then become a mentoring force in their community is significant because it proves that the scholars can learn the basic tenets of a healthy relationship and give and take in positive ways in those relationships.

Possible Responses

- ➤ Implement roundtable meetings in which scholarship students can discuss issues, problems and successes they are facing so far and look to each other for help and advice.
- ➤ Actively encourage students to become mentors for others, perhaps through mentorship workshops or other mentor-focused opportunities in the community.
- ➤ Use the Strength Finder tool to create diversified learning opportunities for the scholars. Strength Finder can be used to assess the scholars' greatest strengths and learning

exercises will help them use those strengths to their greatest potential, to help themselves and their peers.

Finding #8 – "I believe in my future."

All scholars in the program are graduates of Juvenile Court & Community Schools, which serves a student body experiencing extraordinary challenges such as juvenile delinquency, homelessness, community violence and/or teen parenting. Because of this, they are often focused on the present, getting through day-by-day and making sure their basic, immediate needs Through our interviews with participants and mentors, we found that many of the scholars made clear connections between participating in the program and a discovered or renewed focus on their future. In fact, 92% of the students said they now feel more hopeful about their education and future.

Due to the extraordinary circumstances these students come from, scholars often felt as if they were not in control of their own lives but were instead trapped by their upbringing and environment. However, we found that after participating in the program, the financial, mentor and professional development aspects of the program have helped scholars believe in themselves, their futures and their abilities — creating a sense of agency over their personal and academic trajectory. This translates to students taking action toward improving their future.

After participating in the program,

➢ 85% of scholars said they now use coping strategies to address challenges they face

➢ 85% of scholars said they now take action steps toward the goals they set

➢ 100% of scholars said they the now take advantage of academic, professional and community resources

Mentors recognize this growth too:

I think she sees each of these accomplishments as milestones – and they are. It supports her sense of self-worth, value and confidence. For some people, it's easy, but for her it has been incredibly challenging. Every single milestone increases her confidence. And she's facing this hurdle now but she's not going to give up.

Two scholars mentioned they actively plan ahead in terms of applying for additional scholarships, saying, "I'm saving scholarships for further down the line" or "I've been going over my statements more. I figure out when different scholarships are coming in and when the deadlines to apply are." Another shared,

> I had never saved money before and the scholarship program taught me how to…I'm planning on buying a house. Not anytime soon but hopefully in 10 years or so," another scholar said. "I have the skills to save money now and the motivation to buy a house. – *Scholar, age 24*

This same scholar, when asked about how she dealt with challenges, such as persistent mental health issues, throughout her college career said, "I realize I have to focus on my future. The depression and PTSD were because of my past experiences. I learned that I could change things now, so I won't be in the same situation later on. I need to believe in my future."

Significance

At Words Alive, we want participants in all of our programs to become advocates for themselves and their future, especially so in the WAWS program. This finding indicates that through program participation, scholars are learning to proactively contribute to their own personal development by creating long-term goals and that they're making steps towards meeting them. This is not only significant to the individual student but to the larger community. By becoming individuals who are no longer just getting by day-by-day, they are prepared to contribute to local economies, culture, politics, and to help their communities thrive.

Possible Responses
- ➤ Have students fill out a five-year plan.
- ➤ Implement a mentorship log in which mentor and student fill out what they discussed at each meeting. The log will have a "what's next" column to encourage mentors and students to follow through with their plans.
- ➤ Add workshops and exercises about goal setting to the program.

Conclusion

The life challenges that these scholars face as they enter the WAWS program are many and complicated, yet by the end of their time in the program, many scholars view themselves as actors with a set of skills and tools and a defined sense of agency to persevere and achieve anyway. Our research has shown that scholarship funds indeed remove some of the immediate financial barriers to attend school, but it is the personal growth and skillsets to address the challenges of their lives that scholars develop through a cultivated relationship with a mentor that launch them to a new level of what's possible.

Steps Forward
The program adjustments planned for the 2018-19 program year:
- ➤ Standardized financial awards.
- ➤ Stricter, more immediate consequences for scholars when they fail to meet a requirement.
- ➤ Emphasize communication about what is mandatory and what is not. Update Terms & Conditions of the program to include a schedule of deadlines and clear communication about what is mandatory, and have scholars sign it at the orientation. Mentors and scholars retain a copy.
- ➤ Enhanced initial mentor training (through help of The National Mentoring Partnership).
- ➤ Mentors attend quarterly mentor-only meetings for

additional training opportunities, roundtable discussions, etc.

➤ Provide mentorship kit that includes mentor resources, student resources and activities the pair can do together, along with clear program objectives and requirements, etc.

➤ Implement a mentorship log for mentors and their scholars to track their conversations and what needs to be followed up on for each meeting.

➤ Require mentors to attend the scholars' workshops so mentors can ensure knowledge learned is applied.

➤ Provide incentives for students to meet with the mentors regularly.

➤ New scholars in the program must live and attend school in San Diego during their first year in the scholarship program.

➤ Program staff to send birthday cards and other celebratory communication when appropriate.

➤ Continue to diversify learning opportunities for scholars, not only through new workshop opportunities but other cultural opportunities.

Appendix

Qualitative Interview Questions

PeopleShores

What are some of the most significant things you have learnt at PeopleShores? What do you think are some of the long-term benefits of training and working at PeopleShores? How are you thinking differently about your future prospects as a result?

What are some of the core values that you have learnt at PeopleShores? How is the exposure to these values shaping your beliefs about yourselves and community?

What have you become aware of in terms of available support structure (via case worker)? How is having this support system shifted your mindset about dealing with challenges?

What have you become aware of in terms of available support structure (via case worker)? How is having this support system shifted your mindset about dealing with challenges?

What are some of the other personality traits (soft skills) that you are learning? Having the skills and experience, how are you changing personally and professionally? In what way are you actively practicing these values? How is this practice shaping who you are as a leader? (as a professional?)

What have you observed now vs. before in the way you deal with obstacles standing in the way of your goals? How are you growing in the way you deal with challenging situations at or outside of work? In what ways do you feel you still need to grow?

What is the most rewarding part of training and working at PeopleShores? What is tedious? In what way do these experiences shape your overall commitment levels?

What do you enjoy most about the culture and people of PeopleShores? How is this exposure shaping your empathy and gratitude?

When you work at PeopleShores, what kind of emotions do you feel most often? How has the support system you have received here helped you stick with your goals even when the situation was difficult?

Pro Kids | The First Tee of San Diego

What kinds of things made you happiest when you were here (at Pro Kids)? What are you passionate about now that you have graduated from the program?

What is your favorite part of your college/work/professional life? How is that excitement showing up in other areas of your life?

What are ways you stay connected to your community? How have you included community outreach into your busy life?

What improvements did you have to make on the golf-course to become a well-rounded golfer? How have you applied these improvements to other areas in your life or work? How have those improvements helped you evolve as a person?

What have you learned about goal setting? How has that influenced the way you think about your family's future/dreams, what you think is possible for your life?

How did you feel about the community involvement requirement at Pro Kids? What about your community involvement experience has stuck with you?

What kind of knowledge have you gained from working with active support members in your community? How has this shaped the way you think about your role in supporting/shaping/giving back to your community?

What about golf is most difficult/frustrating to you? How do you stay committed during those times when you are frustrated/what keeps you from giving up?

What have you discovered about yourself on the golf course? How have these lessons helped you trust yourself more?

Ronald McDonald House Charitis of Southern California

What have been some of the most significant takeaways (learnings, knowledge nuggets) from your experience at Family Camp? What's still confusing or difficult to warp your mind around? How do you envision these takeaways supporting your child's next steps in their journey?

What memorable activities did you have an opportunity to do together as a family at Family Camp? What steps have you taken (or are you planning to take) to create some of these experiences at home? How have these activities affected your family's dynamic? In what ways, if any, do you think your family has grown?

What insights into your children/family have you gained through your time together at Camp? How have these observations affected your outlook on your family's future? In what ways, if any, does your perspective still need to shift to see the future the way you want (or need) to?

How has being at Family Camp helped to reduce your stress? What still worries or concerns you most? How have you resolved to relieve stress in life as you move forward with your new normal?

What connections have you made through Family Camp that are either new or have grown? How have these connections impacted your family?

What opportunities did you have at Camp to share your cancer journey with others? What opportunities have you had since leaving Camp? In what ways has that impacted your ability to give and accept support from others?

What has been most rewarding for you about reaching out to those families you met once Camp was over? How have those relationships developed/evolved through the years?

Did you come away with any new info that has helped you advocate for your child in new ways? If so, please provide an example/elaborate.

How has Family Camp impacted what excites you about sending your child to Summer Camp? How has it impacted what makes you nervous about sending your child to camp? If you have gained a sense of confidence with sending your child to Camp, how, if at all, has this helped you embrace other unknowns in your child's life?

San Diego Children's Choir

What are some of the most important things you've learned in choir ➔ How has this changed the way you think about yourself as a musician inside and outside of choir? How has this changed the way you think about yourself in general?

What are some of the most challenging aspects of reading music? What are some of the most challenging aspects of being a musician? ➔ What strengths have you developed through choir to help you overcome these challenges? What strengths do you still need to develop to overcome other challenges in music and in life? How has learning these things transformed you as a musician? As a person?

What experiences have you had in choir that have given you the greatest sense of accomplishment? ➔ How have those experiences changed the way you step into your role as a musical artist? How has this changed the way you approach other parts of your life?

What has been your favorite part of choir? ➜ What has it meant for you to be a part of this choir? How has this influenced what you want your life to be about?

What have you been anxious, nervous or worried about prior to or during your time in choir? What has helped you to calm or assure you or give you confidence since you've joined? ➜ How is this shaping your commitment to achieving your goals in music and life?

What have you learned about the music of other cultures? What have you discovered about the differences in music from different cultures? ➜ How has learning about these differences shaped what you think about that culture/community? How has your perspective changed on your culture/community as a result?

What is the toughest thing about working together as a choir? What have you done to overcome these challenges? ➜ How has this helped you build relationships with other chorister's? How has your approach to working with other people changed as you've worked through this?

By being a part of choir, in what ways do you feel more connected to your community? ➜ How has this connectedness shaped your commitment to your fellow chorister and others?

When was one of the first times in choir you had to react to an unexpected situation? What did you learn about yourself through this? ➜ How have these situations changed the way you think about other challenges since then?

What feelings did you experience when you when you succeeded in overcoming the unexpected challenge? ➜ How has this made you more passionate about succeeding in other areas of your life?

What is a non-music specific skill you have learned in choir that you didn't already know? How have you applied this skill? ➜ How has what you've learned here affected you in school? What changes have your teachers, family and friends noticed in you?

Thinking ahead 5-10 years into the future, what does your ideal life look like? What are you doing for school/work and fun? Who is around you? How has your experience in the choir helped you create that ideal life?

Venice Family Clinic

What have you noticed about your involvement in your healthcare since coming to teen clinic? ➜ How has this changed the way you see your role as a part of your healthcare team?

What is still confusing or difficult to understand about your healthcare? How has what you've learned here helping you to work through this? ➜ How has this affected what you believe about your ability to take control of your health?

What challenges have you faced in communicating your health concerns? ➜ How has navigating these challenges changed the way you communicate with your healthcare team and with others in your life?

What are the biggest/most significant changes have you made to improve your health? ➜ In what ways do you still want/need to grow to make more positive changes in your life and the lives of others?

How has your confidence in managing your health changed since coming to teen clinic? ➜ How this made you more dedicated to prioritizing your health?

What emotions do you experience most often about your health? ➜ How is this helping you stick with your commitment to making healthy choices?

Think ahead 3-5 years in your life. If everything goes exactly how you hope it will, what does your ideal life look like? How has your health played a part in (or contributed to) that ideal life? How has what you've learned at the teen clinic helped you make that ideal life a reality?

Words Alive

Questions for Scholars

What lessons have you learned because of your participation in the program? → How has this knowledge impacted your ability to succeed?

What financial habits have you developed since becoming a WAWS scholar? → What changes are you seeing in your life as a result? In what ways are those changes giving you a new set of motivations?

What kind of actions are you taking with your mentor? → How have you applied those actions to other relationships?

How has working with your mentor made you feel? → How do you honor your personal values in your relationship with your mentor?

What strengths and weaknesses have you realized about yourself? → How has your perspective of yourself evolved?

What recurring challenges, if any, are you recognizing as you move along? → What are you realizing you have to believe in order to overcome those challenges?

What has been the most frustrating thing you've learned about yourself in your college career thus far? → How are you dedicated to working through these feelings?

What ideas, principles or passions are you now more eager to express? → How are you staying committed to these ideas, principles or passions even when it's difficult?

What opportunities have you acted on since your participation in WAWS? What did you achieve? → How has that changed the way you will approach your future?

Questions for Mentors

1. What lessons have you seen your mentee learn because of their participation in the program? → How has this knowledge impacted their ability to succeed?

2. What financial habits has your mentee developed since becoming a WAWS scholar? ➜ What changes are you seeing in their life as a result? In what ways are those changes giving them a new set of motivations?

3. What kind of actions does your mentee take in your mentor/mentee relationship? ➜ How has your mentee applied those actions to other relationships?

4. What recurring challenges for your mentee, if any, are you recognizing? ➜ What are you realizing they have to believe in order to overcome those challenges?

5. What opportunities has your mentee acted on since their participation in WAWS? What did they achieve? ➜ How has that changed the way they plan to approach their future?

23889472R00082

Made in the USA
San Bernardino, CA
31 January 2019